Unknowability

Unknowability

An Inquiry into the Limits of Knowledge

NICHOLAS RESCHER

LEXINGTON BOOKS

A Division of
ROWMAN & LITTLEFIELD PUBLISHERS, INC.
Lanham • Boulder • New York • Toronto • Plymouth, UK

LEXINGTON BOOKS

A division of Rowman & Littlefield Publishers, Inc.
A wholly owned subsidary of The Rowman & Littlefield Publishing Group, Inc.
4501 Forbes Boulevard, Suite 200
Lanham, MD 20706

Estover Road
Plymouth PL6 7PY
United Kingdom

British Library Cataloguing in Publication Information Available

Library of Congress Cataloging-in-Publication Data

The hardback edition of this book was previously cataloged by the Library of Congress as
follows:

Rescher, Nicholas.
  Unknowability : an inquiry into the limits of knowledge / Nicholas Rescher.
      p. cm.
  Includes bibliographical references and index.
  1. Knowledge, Theory of. I. Title.
  BD201.R48 2009
  121'.2—dc22   2008056104

ISBN: 978-0-7391-3615-7 (cloth : alk. paper)
ISBN: 978-0-7391-3616-4 (pbk. : alk. paper)
ISBN: 978-0-7391-3662-1 (electronic)

Printed in the United States of America

For Dagfinn Føllesdal

Contents

Preface

The realities of man's cognitive situation are such that our knowledge of the world's ways is bound to be imperfect. Nonetheless, the theory of unknowability—agnoseology as some have called it—is a rather underdeveloped branch of knowledge. And it seems destined to remain so since most of us would prefer to "accentuate the positive" and focus attention on human abilities and powers, rather than disabilities and incapacities.

Granted, the task of identifying individual unknowable facts as such is inherently impracticable. (If they are supposed to be identified as such—as facts—then how can they be unknowable?) But their treatment at the level of generality is something else again. And as the deliberations of the book will endeavor to show in detail, there are four prime reasons for the impracticability of cognitive access to certain facts about the world: developmental impredictability, verificational surdity, ontological detail, and predicative vagrancy. The role of each of these factors will be explained and examined by exploring the prospects and possibilities of knowledge, with particular focus on its limits, practical and theoretical alike.

While my work in epistemology stretches back to the 1950s, during the past decade much of my effort has been dedicated to these themes, and the present book effectively rounds off these investigations.

I am grateful to Estelle Burris for her ever-competent assistance in preparing this material for the press.

1

Unknowable Facts

1. INTRODUCTION

This little book is not an exercise in skepticism; it is not dedicated to the idea
that no one ever knows anything. On the contrary, its approach to knowledge
is far more commonsensical than that, accepting that we know all sorts of
things and that most of the things we take ourselves to know do indeed qual-
ify as authentic knowledge. All the same, there are limits, and it is this that will
be the focus of present concern.

It lies in the nature of the concept that purported *factual* (as opposed to
practical) knowledge is a matter of knowing that something or other is so—
that certain facts obtain. And what is it to be a *fact*? Basically there are two av-
enues to this destination. The one proceeds via the contingent arrangements of
this real world of ours (e.g., "Caesar antedated Napoleon"). The other proceeds
via the logico-conceptual arrangement of ideas (e.g., "blue is a color"). Accordingly, facts are rooted in either the existential or in the logico-conceptual
realities. Assumptions, suppositions, and even postulations do not establish authentic facts but merely *putative* ones.

Then too there is the matter of fiction. In the case of fictions there will certainly be things one cannot know. What was Sherlock Holmes's weight? Did he
have any freckles? The reason for our lack of knowledge is simple. For there just
is no fact of the matter here to serve as an object of knowledge. Where what the

author says does not settle matters, achieving knowledge is impossible because cognition cannot grasp what isn't there. But this sort of unknowability just is not at issue here. Our concern is not with no-fact situations, but with cases where there indeed are facts of the matter but one just cannot get at them. Cognitive inaccessibility to what there is—to fact—is the crux here and unknowing with regard to what is not is beside the point.

All of us are realistic enough to realize that there are facts that we do not know—and many of them: But are there any facts that we *cannot* know—even if that "we" is expanded to included the human race at large?

To be sure, someone may interject as follows: "Suppose that this entire universe of ours were just a subatomic particle in some unimaginably greater megaverse. Surely we would never be able to find that out!" True enough! But also beside the point! For the question that will concern us here is not: "Are there *possible* facts that we could never learn: possibilities which, if they were indeed actualized, would have to remain beyond the reach of our knowledge?" Rather, the question on the agenda of present concern is: "Are any actual facts unknowable—honest to goodness, for-real facts that we cannot possibly get to know?" The issues we propose to investigate lie on the level of actuality—that of imaginative possibility is something else again.

Facts can lie outside a person's cognitive reach for various reasons. These include:

- The individual just is not smart enough to figure it out.
- The information needed for its determination simply is not available.

As to the former, there are puzzles and mathematical problems that will do the trick with most of us. And as to the latter, there is the matter of just how many elephants were alive in Caesar's day. But this sort of things is not at issue here. For there are also facts that are unknowable in principle—for anyone and everyone as a matter of inexorable necessity. It is to this decidedly radical issue of inevitable ignorance that the present deliberations will be addressed. Their concern is not with what we *do not* know, but with what we *cannot* know. And the questions that will preoccupy it are not just questions we cannot answer, but questions which, in the very nature of things, no one can possibly answer.

The idea of *necessary* or *demonstrable* unknowability, this admits of three construals:

- *logical* unknowability—demonstrable on the basis of abstract considerations of epistemic logic.
- *conceptual* unknowability—demonstrable on the basis of an analysis of the salient concept and ideas at issue.
- *in-principle* unknowability—demonstrable on the basis of the fundamental principles that delineate some area of inquiry or deliberation.

Thus it is *logically* demonstrable that one cannot know that such-and-such a particular fact is among those one does not know. It is *unconceptually* impossible to know that a certain idea that has fallen into total oblivion or to know of a particular event that has left no trace of its occurrence. And it is *in-principle* impossible to know when and by whom the word "dog" was first used in English. It is these issues of necessary unknowability that will be at the focus of this book's concerns.

Among the facts that are unknowable are those which relate to the future contingencies of choice and chance. No one can presently identify those who will be killed in next year's automobile accidents; no one can presently identify those whom you will meet en route to the store when next you shop. And this sort of thing holds vis-à-vis the past as well. No one can identify those who are alive today because a certain automobile speed limit was lowered or a certain driver-training program was instituted last year.

This last example takes us into the realm of "but-for" deliberation and here some special considerations come to the fore. For such facts root in counterfactual hypotheses. Thus it may be a fact about the world that John would be dead if he had not jumped out of the way of that onrushing bus. But such iffy "facts" also lie outside the range of our present concern for unknowable fact.

And for very good reason. Thus consider the question: "Would *X* be alive today if *Y* had not introduced his mother to his father?" Well—they could have met in other ways, so that their marriage and *X*'s subsequent birth would be wholly unaffected. But then again, maybe not. And even if *X* was born on schedule, maybe the particular manner of his parents first meeting set in motion a set of events that prevented *X*'s being killed five days ago." The whole question dissolves in an uncharted sea of possibilities and there is no practicable way to navigate in such waters.

So what is one to make of reasoning of the following format?

> If *p* were true, then *XYZ* would be an unknowable fact
> For ought we know *p* might be true
> _____
> Therefore: For ought we know, *XYZ* is an unknowable fact

This inference may look plausible, but it is invalid. The only validly derivable conclusion is:

> Therefore: For ought we know, *XYZ might be* an unknowable fact.

But this "might be" conclusion here eviscerates the reasoning. For a might-be fact just is not a fact—any more than a might-be inheritance is an inheritance or a might-be disaster a disaster.

Granted, one can readily—and quite plausibly—say things on the order of:

> If *XYZ* were a fact, then we could never know it.

Hypothetical unknowability is certainly a prospect. For instance:

> If this entire universe of ours were merely a subatomic
> particle in some unimaginably vast meta-universe, then
> we could never learn about the things that go on there.

But here we are erecting a house of cards on the sand of supposition. What we have is not an unknowable fact but a fact about unknowability—*a conditionally unknowable fact relative to a counterfactual supposition*. This sort of thing is not relevant to the present range of deliberations. Our concern is with unknowable *facts* and not with the unknowable *possibilities* at issue in mere suppositions.

Possibility-mongering does not come to grips with the issues at stake here. Our present concern is with the actualities (and in a way even the inevitabilities) of unknowable fact, not with its possibilities. It is thereby unknowability *as matters stand* that concern us. What would—or might be—unknowable if certain weird conditions obtained is not a matter of present concern.

For present purposes, however, all this is immaterial. Our present concern is with *actual facts*. Unknowability in the context of hypothetical or conjectural possibilities is something else again, beside the point of present concern.

One can certainly know *that* something or other is possible, but that which is *merely* possible but not actual for this very reason is something that one cannot know to be so.[1]

2. UNKNOWABILITY

The great American philosopher C. S. Peirce wrote:

> For my part, I cannot admit the proposition of Kant—that there are certain impassable bounds to human knowledge. . . . The history of science affords illustrations enough of the folly of saying that this, that, or the other can never be found out. Auguste Comte said that it was clearly impossible for man ever to learn anything of the chemical constitution of the fixed stars, but before his book had reached its readers the discovery which he had announced as impossible had been made. Legendre said of a certain proposition in the theory of numbers that, while it appeared to be true, it was most likely beyond the powers of the human mind to prove it; yet the next writer on the subject gave six independent demonstrations of the theorem.[2]

The present discussion will argue that, notwithstanding the plausibility of Peirce's considerations, there indeed are some impassable bounds to human knowledge.

To be sure, there is a perverse sense in which there are no statements whose truths-status is undecidable and no questions that are unanswerable. For you can of course decide for or against statements by merely flipping a coin. And you can answer every question by the simple algorithm that if the question asks *why?* you answer "Because God wants it that way"; if the question asks *when?* you say "yesterday"; if the question asks *where?* you say "In Paris"; and so on. You need never be at a loss for words. But of course what is wanted in these matters is not just a decision but a rationally grounded decision and not just an answer—even one that happens to be correct—but one whose correctness can be made manifest. The crux throughout is a matter of rational cogency.

There are two modes of personal ignorance: the culpable and the inevitable. Culpable ignorance exists when one should know something but doesn't; inevitable ignorance exists where there just is no possible way of knowing something. The necessary unknowability that concerns us here invariably falls into the latter range.

Here we are not interested in questions whose unanswerability resides merely in the contingent fact that certain information is not in practice accessible. The present deliberations do not concern the contingent cognitive limitations of individuals, but rather those deeply intractable issues that no one can possibly resolve as a matter of principle rather than contingent circumstance. (No one knows what Caesar ate for breakfast on that fatal Ides of March—but that is so simply because there is no way in which we can secure the needed information here and now.) The crux, rather, is a matter of the inevitable inhabitability of questions that are unanswerable as a matter of principle.

Now when some fact is said to be unknowable, the question will immediately arise: for whom? And there are various prospects here, specifically:

- for a given individual
- for humans in general
- for finite intelligent beings at large

It will, ultimately, be this last and strongest mode of unknowability that constitutes the focus of these present deliberations.

As regards those facts that are unknowable only for a particular individual, consider an example. There are (surely) various facts that you do not know. But the truth of a specific claim of the format "F is a fact that I do not know" is something you cannot possibly know. To do so, you would have to know that F is a fact—which is exactly what is now being denied. "What is an example of a fact that you do not know?" is a question you cannot possibly answer correctly (though others will have no difficulty with it).[3] For "F is a fact I do not know" is self-contradicting in its claim to F's factuality. And much the same holds of the claim "B is a belief I (now) hold mistakenly." Such contentions are self-negating. What the one hand gives, the other takes away.

But more far-reachingly, there are also facts that no one can possibly know—issues whose resolution lies beyond the power of anyone and everyone. Given human finitude—both at the level of individuals and collectively—there will be some facts which nobody actually knows so that the now-generalized question "What is an example of a fact that nobody knows?" will be unanswerable. For while it doubtless has an answer, it will nevertheless be one that no one can appropriately provide, since that such-and-such a particular fact is universally unknown to be so is something that no one can possibly know. Yet while it is obviously impossible to provide examples of unknowable facts, it would take considerable hubris to deny that such facts exist. Thus if no intelligent being in the cosmos happens to know that a certain fact obtains, then nobody can know that this particular circumstance is so. Even as our own ignorance lies outside our personal ken, so our collective ignorance lies outside our collective ken as well. If altogether untenable facts are there, then nobody can know this in detail. There are bound to be regions of our ignorance to which knowledge can gain no access.

Can anything general be said regarding just what it is that those unknowable facts are about?

The principal categories of classical ontology are:

- *transcendentalia*: God, angels, the extra-mundane
- *realia*: real things existing in the world
- *absracta*: abstract conceptual items, especially mathematical objects
- *possibilia*: unrealized possibilities
- *fictionalia*: fictional objects

Now as already noted, fictionalia fall outside the range of present deliberations because our present topic is to be unknowabiltiy in relation to matters of mundane fact. And this also puts transcendentals aside of our present concerns, notwithstanding the fact that theologians here generally insisted upon the unknowability of God. Moreover, as just noted for the same reason, possibilia also fall outside our scope. Then too we shall not here address (more that illustratively) the issue of unknowable abstract/mathematical fact and issues of indemonstrability in the abstract sciences where knowledge proceeds through demonstration.[4] Our present focus is to be on issues of unknowability about reality—about the facts of the world.

3. UNKNOWABLE FACTS VERSUS UNANSWERABLE QUESTIONS

An important indicator of limits to knowledge lies in the consideration that not only are there questions that cannot be answered cogently, but there will also be questions that one cannot even pose. Julius Caesar could not have wondered if his sword contained tungsten or if Rutherford B. Hayes won the U.S. presidency legally. The very concepts needed to form such question are outside the conceptual horizons of people at some times and places—or possibly of people at all times and places. And just such conceptual horizons afford a key pathway to the unknowable.

There are bound to be regions of our ignorance to which knowledge can gain no access, seeing that it is beyond the limits of possibility for anyone to know the details of their ignorance. To elucidate this idea, it is instructive to adopt an erotetic—that is, question-oriented—view of knowledge and ignorance.

It can be supposed, without loss of generality, that the answers to factual questions are always complete propositions. Thus consider such examples as:

Q. "Who is that Man?"

A. "Tom Jones."

Q. "When will he come?"

A. "At two o'clock."

Q. "What prime numbers lie between two and eight?"

A. "Three, five, and seven."

Throughout, the answers can be recast in the form of completed propositions, respectively: "That man is Tom Jones"; "He will come at two o'clock"; "Three, five, and seven are the prime numbers between two and eight." So we shall here take the line that proper answers to questions are given as complete propositions.

Furthermore, it must be acknowledged that *answering* a question is not simply a matter of giving a response that happens to be correct. For a proper answer must not be just correct but also credible: it must have the backing of a rationale that renders its correctness evident. For example, take the question whether the mayor of San Antonio had eggs for breakfast yesterday. You say yes, I say no—though neither of us has a clue. One of us is bound to be right. But neither one of us has managed to provide an actual answer to the question. One of us has made a verbal response that happens to be correct, but neither of us has given a cognitively appropriate answer in the sense of the term that is now at issue. For that would require the backing of a cogent rationale of credibility; merely to guess at an answer, for example, or to draw it out of a hat, is not really to provide one.

And now back to our main theme. The most emphatically unanswerable questions are those which a particular individual or group is unable to answer. An instance of such a question is: "What is an example of a fact of which you are altogether ignorant?" Clearly you cannot possibly manage to answer this, because whatever you adduce as such a fact must be something you know or believe to be such (that is, a fact), so that you cannot possibly be altogether ignorant of it. On the other hand, it is clear that *somebody else* could readily be in the position to answer the question. Again, consider such questions as:

- What is an example of a problem that will never be considered by any human being?
- What is an example of an idea that will never occur to any human being?

There are sound reasons of general principle (the potential infinitude of problems and ideas; the inherent finitude of human intelligence) to hold that the items at issue in these questions (problems that will never be considered; ideas that will never occur) do actually exist. And it seems altogether plausible to think that other (nonhuman) hypothetically envisionable intelligences could well answer these questions correctly. But it is equally clear that we humans could never provide the requisite answers.

And looking beyond this we can also contemplate the prospect of globally intractable questions such that no one (among finite intelligences at least) can possibly be in a position to answer them correctly. These questions have an appropriate answer but for reasons of general principle no one—no finite intelligence at least—can possibly be in a position to provide it. An example of such globally unanswerable questions can be provided by nontrivial but yet inherently uninstantiable predicates along the lines of

- "What idea is there that has never occurred to anybody?"
- "What occurrence is there that no one ever mentions?"

There undoubtedly are such items, but of course they cannot be instantiated, so that questions which ask for examples here are inherently unanswerable.[5]

Analogously, one can ask if there are any unspecifiable truths.

As these considerations indicate, questions about the limits of our factual knowledge are particularly intractable. And indeed the issue of the extent of our cognitive incapacity is itself perhaps the most dramatic and fateful token of the limits of human knowledge.

NOTES

1. While $K\Diamond p$ is perfectly coherent, nevertheless $\Diamond p$ & $\sim pi$ is inconsistent with Kp (seeing that $Kp \rightarrow p$).

2. Charles Sanders Peirce, *Collected Papers,* ed. by C. Hartshorne et al., vol. VI (Cambridge, Mass.: Harvard University Press, 1929), sect. 6.556.

3. There is, of course, no earthly reason why you cannot know that F is a fact that I do not know. It's just that I cannot possibly manage it. And this is so not for factual reasons relative to my stupidity but for conceptual reasons relating to the nature of the knowledge-claim that would be at issue.

4. On the mathematical issues see Gregory J. Chaitin, *The Unknowable* (Singapore; New York: Springer, 1999).

5. This issue here is one of so-called *vagrant* predicates that have no known address.

2

Future Knowledge and Its Problems

1. ISSUES OF FUTURE KNOWLEDGE

The issue of future knowledge is particularly significant for the theme of unknowability. For here the knowledge-frustrating factors of choice and chance come into operation with special force. Philosophers since Aristotle have stressed that knowledge about the future poses drastic problems.[1] No one can possibly predict today what the discoveries of tomorrow will be. To be sure, there is no inherent problem about predicting *that* a certain discovery will be made. But *how* it will be made is altogether unfathomable. After all, if we could solve tomorrow's problems today they simply would not be tomorrow's problems.

Any state of science delimits the range of legitimately posable questions to those whose presuppositions it can endorse. If quantum theory is right, the position and velocity of certain particles cannot be pinpointed conjointly. This renders the question "What is the exact position and velocity of particle X at time t?" not insoluble but illegitimate. Question-illegitimacy represents a limit that grows out of science itself—a limit on appropriate questions rather than on available solutions. Insolubilia, however, are something very different: they are legitimate questions to which no answer can possibly be given—*now or ever.*

Any claim to identify insolubilia by pinpointing here and now scientific questions that science will *never* resolve is bound to be problematic—indeed, extremely far-fetched. For to identify an issue as insoluble, we would have to show that a certain scientifically appropriate question is such that its resolution lies beyond every (possible or imaginable) state of future science. This is clearly a *very* tall order—particularly so in view of our inevitably deficient grasp on future states of science. After all, how could we possibly establish that a question *Q* will continue to be *raisable and unanswerable* in every future state of science, seeing that we cannot now circumscribe the changes that science might undergo in the future? We would have to argue that the answer to *Q* lies "in principle" beyond the reach of science. And this would gravely compromise the legitimacy of the question as a genuinely scientific one. For if the question is such that its resolution lies *in principle* beyond the powers of science, it is difficult to see how one could maintain it to be an authentic scientific question.

After all, that aspect of the future which is most evidently unknowable is the future of invention, of discovery, of innovation—and particularly in the case of science itself. As Immanuel Kant insisted long ago that every new discovery opens the way to others, every question that is answered gives rise to yet further questions to be investigated.[2] The present state of science can never answer definitively from that of the future, since it cannot even predict what questions lie in the agenda.

We certainly cannot foresee what we cannot even conceive. Our questions—let alone answers—cannot outreach the limited horizons of our concepts. Having never contemplated electronic computing machines as such, the ancient Romans could also venture no predictions about their impact on the social and economic life of the twenty-first century. Clever though he unquestionably was, Aristotle could not have pondered the issues of quantum electrodynamics. The scientific questions of the future are—at least in part—bound to be conceptually inaccessible to the inquirers of the present. The question of just how the cognitive agenda of some future date will be constituted is clearly irresolvable for us now. Not only can we not anticipate future discoveries now, we cannot even pre-discern the questions that will arise as time moves on and cognitive progress with it.[3]

Investigation and inquiry are ventures in innovation. And in consequence it lies in the nature of things that present science can never speak decisively for future science, and present science cannot predict the specific discoveries of future inquiry. After all, our knowledge of the present cannot encompass that of the future—if we could know about those future discoveries now they would not have to await the future. Accordingly, knowledge about what rational inquiry will achieve over all—and thus just where it will be going in the long run—are beyond the reach of attainable knowledge at this or any other particular stage of the cognitive "state of the art."

After all, it is in principle infeasible for us to tell not only how future science will answer present questions but even what questions will figure on the question agenda of the future, let alone what answers they will engender. In this regards, as in others, it lies in the inevitable realities of our condition that the details of our ignorance are—for us at least—hidden away in an impenetrable fog of obscurity.

2. DIFFICULTIES IN PREDICTING FUTURE SCIENCE

The landscape of natural science is ever-changing: innovation is the very name of the game. Not only do the theses and themes of science change but so do the very questions.

In inquiry, as in other areas of human affairs, major upheavals can come about in a manner that is sudden, unanticipated, and often unwelcome. Major scientific breakthroughs often result from research projects that have very different ends in view. Louis Pasteur's discovery of the protective efficacy of inoculation with weakened disease strains affords a striking example. While studying chicken cholera, Pasteur accidentally inoculated a group of chickens with a weak culture. The chickens became ill, but, instead of dying, recovered. Pasteur later reinoculated these chickens with fresh culture—one strong enough to kill an ordinary chicken. To Pasteur's surprise, the chickens remained healthy. Pasteur then shifted his attention to this interesting phenomenon, and a productive new line of investigation opened up. In empirical inquiry, we generally cannot tell in advance what further questions will be engendered by our endeavors to answer those on hand. New scientific questions arise from answers we give to previous ones, and thus the issues of future science simply lie beyond our present horizons.

One would certainly like to be in a position to have prior insight into and give some advance guidance to the development of scientific progress. But grave difficulties arise where questions about the future, and in particular the *cognitive* future, are involved.

When the prediction of a specific predefined occurrence is at issue, a forecast can go wrong in only one way: by proving to be incorrect. The particular development in question may simply not happen as predicted. But the forecasting of a general course of developments can go wrong in two ways: either through errors of commission (that is, forecasting something quite different from what actually happens—say, a rainy season instead of a drought), or through errors of omission (that is, failing to foresee some significant part of the overall course—predicting an outbreak of epidemic, say, without recognizing that one's own locality will be involved). In the first case, one forecasts the wrong thing; in the second, there is a lack of completeness, a failure of prevision, a certain blindness.

In cognitive forecasting, it is the errors of omission—our blind spot, as it were—that present the most serious threat. For the fact is that we cannot substantially anticipate the evolution of knowledge.

We cannot tell in advance what the specific answers to our scientific questions will be. It would, after all, be quite unreasonable to expect detailed prognostications about the particular *content* of scientific discoveries. It may be possible in some cases to speculate that science will solve a certain problem, but *how* it will do so lies beyond the ken of those who antedate the discovery itself. If we could *predict* discoveries in detail in advance, then we could *make* them in advance.[4] In matters of scientific importance, then, we must be prepared for surprises. Commenting shortly after the publication of Frederick Soddy's speculations about atomic bombs in his 1920 book *Science and Life*, Robert A. Millikan, a Nobel laureate in physics, wrote that "the new evidence born of further scientific study is to the effect that it is highly improbable that there is any appreciable amount of available subatomic energy to tap."[5] In science forecasting, the record of even the most qualified practitioners is poor.

It is a key fact of life that ongoing progress in scientific inquiry is a process of *conceptual* innovation that always places certain developments outside the cognitive horizons of earlier workers because the very concepts operative in their characterization become available only in the course of scientific discovery itself. (Short of learning our science from the group up, Aristotle could have made nothing of modern genetics, nor Newton of quantum physics.) The major discoveries of later stages are ones which the workers of a substantially earlier period (however clever) not only have failed to make but which they could not even have *understood*, because the requisite concepts were simply not available to them.

An ironic but critically important feature of scientific inquiry is that the unforeseeable tends to be of special significance just because of its unpredictability. The more important the innovation, the less predictable it is, because its very unpredictability is a key index of importance. Science forecasting is beset by a pervasive *normality bias*, because the really novel often seems so bizarre. A. N. Whitehead has wisely remarked:

> If you have had your attention directed to the novelties in thought in your own lifetime, you will have observed that almost all really new ideas have a certain aspect of foolishness when they are first produced.[6]

Before the event, revolutionary scientific innovations will, if imaginable at all, generally be deemed outlandishly wild speculation—mere science fiction, or perhaps just plain craziness.[7]

However, in maintaining that future science is inherently unpredictable, one must be careful to keep in view the distinction between substantive and structural issues, between particular individual scientific questions, theses, and theories, and generic features of the entire system of such individual items. At the level of loose generality, various inductions regarding the future of science can no doubt be safely made. We can, for example, confidently predict that future science will have greater taxonomic diversification, greater theoretical unification, greater substantive complexity, further high-level unification and low-level proliferation, increased taxonomic speciation of subject-matter specialties, and so on. And we can certainly predict that it will be incomplete, that its agenda of availably open questions will be extensive, and so on. But of course this sort of information tells us only about the structure of future science, and not about its *substance*. These structural generalities do not bear on the level of substantive detail: they relate to science as a productive *enterprise* (or "industry) rather than as a substantive *discipline* (as the source of specific theories about the workings of nature).

With respect to the major substantive issues of future natural science, we must be prepared for the unexpected. We can confidently say of future science *that* it will do its job of prediction and control better than ours; but we do not—and in the very nature of things cannot—know *how* it will go about this.

3. PRESENT SCIENCE CANNOT SPEAK FOR FUTURE SCIENCE

Analysis of the theoretical general principles of the case and induction from the history of science both indicate that the theories accepted at one stage of scientific inquiry need not carry over to another but can be replaced by something radically different. The reality of past scientific revolutions cannot be questioned, and the prospect of future scientific revolutions cannot be precluded. Yet it lies in the nature of things that we cannot pinpoint them. The substance of future science inevitably lies beyond our present grasp.

If there was one thing of which the science of the first half of the seventeenth century was confident, it was that natural processes are based on contact-interaction and that there can be no such thing as action at a distance. Newtonian gravitation burst upon this scene like a bombshell. Newton's supporters simply stonewalled. Roger Cotes explicitly denied there was a problem, arguing (in his Preface to the second edition of Newton's *Principia*) that nature was *generally* unintelligible, so that the unintelligibility of forces acting without contact was nothing specifically worrisome. However unpalatable Cotes's position may seem as a precept for science (given that making nature's workings understandable is, after all, one of the aims of the enterprise), there is something to be said for it—not, to be sure, as science but as metascience. For we cannot hold the science of tomorrow bound to the standards of intelligibility espoused by the science of today. The cognitive future is inaccessible to even the ablest of present-day workers. After Pasteur had shown that bacteria could come only from preexisting bacteria, Darwin wrote that "it is mere rubbish thinking of the origin of life; one might as well think of the origin of matter."[8] One might indeed!

The inherent unpredictability of future scientific developments—the fact that no secure inference can be drawn from one state of science to another—has important implications for the issue of the limits of science. It means that present-day science cannot speak for future science: it is in principle impossible to make any secure inferences from the substance of science at one time about its substance at a significantly different time. The prospect of future scientific revolutions can never be precluded. We cannot say with unblinking confidence what sorts of resources and conceptions the science of the future will or will not use. Given that it is effectively impossible to predict the details of what future science will accomplish, it is no less impossible to predict in detail what future science will *not* accomplish. We can never confidently put this or that range of issues outside "the limits of science," because we cannot discern the shape and substance of future science with sufficient clarity to be able to say with any assurance what it can and cannot do. Any attempt to set "limits" to science—any advance specification of what science can and cannot do by way of handling problems and solving questions—is destined to come to grief.

An apparent violation of the rule that present science cannot bind future science is afforded by John von Neumann's attempt to demonstrate that all future theories of subatomic phenomena—and thus all *future* theories—will have to contain an analogue of Heisenber's uncertainty principle if they are to account for the data explained by present theory. Complete predictability at the subatomic level, he argued, was thus exiled from science. But the "demonstration" proposed by von Neumann in 1932 places a substantial burden on potentially changeable details of presently accepted theory.[9] The fact remains that we cannot preclude fundamental innovation in science: present theory cannot delimit the potential of future discovery. In natural science we cannot erect our structures with a solidity that defies demolition and reconstruction. Even if the existing body of "knowledge" does confidently and unqualifiedly support a certain position, this circumstance can never be viewed as absolutely final. The long and short of it is that no one claims with confidence that the science of tomorrow will resolve the issues that the science of today sees as intractable. Present science can issue no guarantees for future science.

4. THE PLASTICITY OF SCIENCE

The *supremacy* of natural science in its own domain is closely bound up with its *plasticity*. If we could set limits to the shape and substance of science, then it would also be possible to set limits to what science can and cannot accomplish. But this is simply impracticable.

For while we can indeed say with confidence what the state of science *as we now have it* does and does not allow, we cannot say what science as such will or will not allow. The boundary between the tenable and the untenable in science is never easy to discern. We certainly cannot defensibly project the present lineaments of science into the future. Future science can turn in unexpected and implausible directions.

Natural science is simply too opportunistic to be fastidious about its mechanisms: eighteenth-century psychologists ruled out hypnotism; nineteenth-century biologists excluded geophysical catastrophes. Twentieth-century

geologists long rejected continental drift. Many contemporary scientists give
parapsychology short shrift—yet who can say that its day will never come? The
pivotal issue is not what is substantively claimed by an assertion but rather
whether this assertion (whatever its content!) has been substantiated by the
prevailing canons of scientific method.

There is, to be sure, rough wisdom in scientific caution and conservatism:
it is perfectly appropriate to be skeptical about unusual phenomena-con-
structions and to view them with skepticism. Before admitting "strange" phenomena as appropriate exploratory issues, we certainly want to check their
credentials, make sure they are well attested and appropriately characterized.
The very fact that they go against our understanding of nature's ways (as best
we can tell) renders abnormalities suspect—a proper focus of worriment and
distrust. But, of course, to hew this line dogmatically and rigidly, in season and
out, is a mistake. The untenable in science does not conveniently wear its untenability on its sleeves. We have to realize that, throughout the history of science, stumbling on anomalies—on "strange phenomena," occurrences that
just don't fit into the existing framework—has been a strong force of scientific
progress.

One does well to distinguish two modes of "strangeness": the exotic and the
counterindicated. The *exotic* is simply something foreign—something that
does not fall into the range of what is known but does not clash with it either.
It lies in what would otherwise be an informational vacuum, *outside* our current understanding of the natural order. (Hypnotism and precognition are
perhaps cases in point.) The *counterindicated*, however, stands in actual *conflict* with our current understanding of the natural order (action at a distance
for seventeenth-century physics; telekinesis today).

Now granted, one would certainly want to apply rigid standards of recognition and admission to phenomena that are counterindicated. But if and
when they measure up, we have to take them in our stride. In science we have
no alternative but to follow nature where it leads. And new theories can be
ruled out even less than new phenomena, for to do so would be to claim that
science has reached the end of its tether, something we certainly cannot and
doubtless should not even wish to do. The task of specifying the limits of scientific capability in the production of knowledge is itself one that transcends
the limits of our cognitive powers.

NOTES

1. That contingent future developments are by nature cognitively intractable, even for God, was a favored theme among the medieval scholastics. On this issue see Marilyn McCord Adams, *William Ockham*, vol. II (Notre Dame, Ind.: University of Notre Dame Press, 1987), chap. 27.

2. On this theme see the author's *Kant and the Reach of Reason: Studies in Kant's Theory of Rational Systematization* (Cambridge: Cambridge University Press, 2000).

3. Of course these questions already exist—what lies in the future is not their existence but their presence on the agenda of active concern.

4. As one commentator has wisely written: "But prediction in the field of pure science is another matter. The scientist sets forth over an uncharted sea and the scribe, left behind on the dock is asked what he may find at the other side of the waters. If the scribe knew, the scientist would not have to make his voyage" (Anonymous, "The Future as Suggested by Developments of the Past Seventy-Five Years," *Scientific American* 123 [1920], 321).

5. Quoted in *Daedalus* 107 (1978), 24.

6. A. N. Whitehead, as cited in John Ziman, *Reliable Knowledge* (Cambridge: Cambridge University Press, 1969), 142–43.

7. See Thomas Kuhn, *The Structure of Scientific Revolution*, 2nd ed. (Chicago: University of Chicago Press, 1970), for an interesting development of the normal/revolutionary distinction.

8. Quoted in Philip Handler, ed., *Biology and the Future of Man* (Oxford: Oxford University Press, 1970), 165.

9. See also the criticisms of his argument in David Bohm, *Causality and Chance in Modern Physics* (London: Routledge, 1957), 95–96.

3

Problems of Alien Cognition

1. ALIEN SCIENCE

To get a better grip on the idea of unknowable facts, it is helpful to consider in prospect the cognitive situation of an astronomically remote alien civilization. What would the "science" of such a civilization be like?

To begin with, there is the question of just what it means for there to be another science-possessing civilization. Note that this is a question that *we* are putting—a question posed in with reference to our understanding of what it means to be a "science." It pivots on the issue of whether *we* would be prepared to consider certain of *their* activities—once we duly understood them—as engaged in scientific inquiry, and whether *we* would be prepared to recognize the product of their activities as constituting a (state of a branch of) science.

Accordingly, a scientific civilization is not merely one that possesses intelligence and social organization but one that puts this intelligence and organization to work in a very particular way by cultivating the enterprise we call *science.* This pens up a rather subtle issue of priority in regard to process versus product. Is what counts for a civilization's "having a science" primarily a matter of the substantive *content* of their doctrines (their belief structures and theory complexes), or is it primarily a matter of the *aims and purposes* with which their doctrines are formed?

The matter of substantive content turns on the issue of how similar their scientific beliefs are to ours, which is clearly something on which we would be ill advised to put much emphasis. After all, the speculations of the nature-theorists of pre-Socratic Greece, our ultimate ancestors in the scientific enterprise, bear little resemblance to our present-day sciences, nor does the content of contemporary physics bear all that much resemblance to that of Newton's day. We would do better to give prime emphasis to matters of process and purpose.

Accordingly, the matter of these aliens "having a science" is to be regarded as turning not on the extent to which their *findings* resemble ours but on the extent to which their *project* resembles ours: we must decide whether we are engaged in the same sort of rational inquiry in terms of the sorts of issues being addressed and the ways in which they are going about addressing them. The issue is at bottom not one of the *substantive similarity* of their "science" to ours but one of the *functional equivalency* of their projects to the scientific enterprise as we know it. Only if they are pursuing such goals as description, explanation, prediction, and control of nature will they be doing *science.*

2. THE POTENTIAL DIVERSITY OF "SCIENCE"
To what extent would the *functional equivalent* of natural science built up by the inquiring intelligences of an astronomically remote civilization be bound to resemble our science? In reflecting on this question and its ramifications, one soon comes to realize that there is an enormous potential for diversity.

To begin with, the *machinery of formulation* used in expressing their science might be altogether different. Specifically, their mathematics might be very unlike ours. Their dealings with quantity might be entirely anumerical—purely comparative, for example, rather than quantitative. Especially if their environment is not amply endowed with solid objects or stable structures congenial to measurement—if, for example, they were jellyfish-like creatures swimming about in a soupy sea—their "geometry" could be something rather strange, largely topological, say, and geared to flexible structures rather than fixed sizes or shapes. Digital thinking might be undeveloped, while certain sorts of analog reasoning might be highly refined. Or, again, an alien civilization might, like the ancient Greeks, have "Euclidean" geometry without analysis. In any case, given that the mathematical mechanisms at their disposal could be very different from ours, it is clear that their description of nature in mathematical terms could also be very different (not necessarily truer or false, but just different).

Secondly, the *orientation* of the science of an alien civilization might be very different. All their efforts might conceivably be devoted to the social sciences—to developing highly sophisticated analogues of psychology and sociology, for example. In particular, if the intelligent aliens were a diffuse assemblage of units comprising wholes in ways that allow for overlap,[1] then the rile of social concepts might become so paramount for them that nature would throughout be viewed in fundamentally social categories, with those aggregates we think of as physical structures contemplated by them in social terms.

Then, too, their natural science might deploy *explanatory mechanisms* very different from ours. Communicating by some sort of "telepathy" based upon variable odors or otherwise "exotic" signals, they might devise a complex theory of emphatic thought-wave transmittal through an ideaferous aether. Again, the aliens might scan nature very differently. Electromagnetic phenomena might lie altogether outside the ken of alien life forms; if their environment does not afford them lodestone and electrical storms, the occasion to develop electromagnetic theory might never arise. The course of scientific development tends to flow in the channel of practical interests. A society of porpoises might lack crystallography but develop a very sophisticated hydrodynamics; one comprised of mole-like creatures might never dream of developing optics or astronomy. One's language and thought processes are bound to be closely geared to the world as one experiences it. As is illustrated by the difficulties we ourselves have in bringing the language of everyday experience to bear on subatomic phenomena, our concepts are ill attuned to facets of nature different in scale or structure from our own. We can hardly expect a "science" that reflects such parochial preoccupations to be a universal fixture.

The interests of creatures shaped under the remorseless pressure of evolutionary adaptations to very different—and endlessly variable—environmental conditions might well be oriented in directions very different from anything that is familiar to us.

Laws reflect detectable regularities in nature. But detection will of course vary drastically with the mode of observations—that is, with the sort of resources that different creatures have at their disposal to do their detecting. Everything depends on how nature pushes back upon our senses and their instrumental extensions. Even if we detect everything we can, we will not have gotten hold of everything available to others. And the converse is equally true.

The laws that we (or anybody else) manage to formulate will depend crucially on one's place within nature—on how one is connected into its wiring diagram, so to speak.

A comparison of the "science" of different civilizations here on earth suggests that it is not an outlandish hypothesis to suppose that the very *topics* of alien science might differ dramatically from those of ours. In our own case, for example, the fact that we live on the surface of the earth (unlike whales), the fact that we have eyes (unlike worms) and thus can *see* the heavens, the fact that we are so situated that the seasonal positions of heavenly bodies are intricately connected with agriculture—all these facts are clearly connected with the development of astronomy. The fact that those distant creatures would experience nature in ways very different from ourselves means that they can be expected to raise very different sorts of questions. Indeed, the mode of emplacement within the nature of alien inquirers might be so different as to focus their attention on entirely different aspects of constituents of the cosmos. If the world is sufficiently complex and multifaceted, they might concentrate upon aspects of their environment that mean nothing to us, with the result that their natural science is oriented in directions very different from ours.[2]

Moreover, the *conceptualization* of an alien science might be very different, for we must reckon with the theoretical possibility that a remote civilization might operate with a drastically different system of concepts in its cognitive dealings with nature. Different cultures and different intellectual traditions, to say nothing of different sorts of creatures, are bound to describe and explain their experience—their world as they conceive it—in terms of concepts and categories of understanding substantially different from ours. They would diverge radically with respect to what the Germans call their *Denkmittel*—the conceptual—instruments they employ in thought about the facts (or purported facts) of the world. They could, accordingly, be said to operate with different conceptual schemes, with different conceptual tools used to "make sense" of experience—to characterize, describe, and explain the items that figure in the world as they view it. The taxonomic and explanatory mechanisms by means of which their cognitive business is transacted might differ so radically from ours that intellectual contact with them would be difficult or impossible.

Epistemologists have often said things to the effect that people whose experience of the world is substantially different from our own are bound to conceive of it in very different terms. Sociologists, anthropologists, and linguists talk in much the same terms, and philosophers of science have recently also come to say the same sorts of things. According to Thomas Kuhn, for example, scientists who work within different scientific traditions—and thus operate with different descriptive and explanatory "paradigms"—actually "live in different worlds."[3]

It is (or should be) clear that there is no single, unique, ideally adequate concept-framework for "describing the world." The botanist, horticulturists, landscape gardener, farmer, and painter will operate from diverse cognitive "points of view" to describe one selfsame vegetable garden. It is merely mythology to think that the "phenomena of nature" can lend themselves to only one correct style of descriptive and explanatory conceptualizations. There is surely no "ideal scientific language" that has a privileged status for the characterization of reality. Different sorts of creatures are bound to make use of different conceptual schemes for the representation of their experience. To insist on the ultimate uniqueness of science is to succumb to "the myth of the God's-eye view." Different cognitive perspectives are possible, not one of them more adequate or more correct than any other independently of the aims and purposes of their users.

Supporting considerations for this position have been advanced from very different points of view. One example is a *Gedankenexperiment* suggested by Georg Simmel in the last century, which envisaged an entirely different sort of cognitive being: intelligent and actively inquiring creatures (animals, say, or beings from outer space) whose experiential modes are quite different from our own.[4] Their senses respond rather differently to physical influences: they are relatively insensitive, say, to heat and light, but substantially sensitized to various electromagnetic phenomena. Such intelligent creatures, Simmel held, could plausibly be supposed to operate within a largely different framework of empirical concepts and categories; the events and objects of the world of their experience might be very different from those of our own: their phenomenological predicates, for example, might have altogether variant descriptive domains. In a similar vein, Williams James wrote:

> Were we lobsters, or bees, it might be that our organization would have led to our using quite different modes from these [actual ones] of apprehending our experiences. It *might* be too (we cannot dogmatically deny this) that such categories unimaginable by us to-day, would have proved on the whole as serviceable for handling our experiences mentally as those we actually use.[5]

The science of a different civilization would inevitably be closely tied to the particular pattern of their interaction with nature as funneled through the particular course of their evolutionary adjustment to their specific environment. The "forms of sensibility" of radically different beings (to invoke Kant's useful idea) are likely to be radically diverse from ours. The direct chemical analysis of environmental materials might prove highly useful, and bioanalytic techniques akin to our senses to taste and smell could be very highly developed, providing them with environmentally oriented "experiences" of a very different sort.

The constitution of alien inquirers—physical, biological, and social—thus emerges as crucial for science. It would be bound to condition the agenda of questions and the instrumentalities for their resolution—to fix what is seen as interesting, important, relevant, and significant. Because it determines what is seen as an appropriate question and what is judged as an admissible solution, the cognitive posture of the inquirers must be expected to play a crucial role in shaping the course of scientific inquiry itself.

To clarify this idea of a conceptually different science, it helps to cast the issue in temporal rather than spatial terms. The descriptive characterization of *alien* science is a project rather akin in its difficulty to that of describing our own *future* science. It is a key fact of life that progress in science is a process of *ideational* innovation that always places certain developments outside the intellectual horizons of earlier workers. The very concepts we think in terms of become available only in the course of scientific discovery itself. Like the science of the remote future, the science of remote aliens must be presumed to be such that we really could not achieve intellectual access to it on the basis of our own position in the cognitive scheme of things. Just as the technology of a more advanced civilization would be bound to strike us as magic, so its science would be bound to strike us as incomprehensible gibberish—until we had learned it "from the ground up." They might (just barely) be able to *teach* it to us, but they could not *explain* it to us by transposing it into our terms.

The most characteristic and significant difference between one conceptual scheme and another arises when the one scheme is committed to something the other does not envisage at all—something that lies outside the conceptual range of the other. A typical case is that of the stance of Cicero's thought-world with regard to questions of quantum electrodynamics. The Romans of classical antiquity did not hold *different* views on these issues; they held no view at all about them. This whole set of relevant considerations remained outside their conceptual repertoire. The diversified history of *our* terrestrial science gives one some minuscule inkling of the vast range of possibilities along these lines.

The "science" of different civilizations may well, like Galenic and Pasteurian medicine, simply *change the subject* in key respects so as to no longer "talk about the same things," but deal with materials (e.g., humors and bacteria, respectively) of which the other take no cognizance at all. The difference in regard to the "conceptual scheme" between modern and Galenic medicine is not that the modern physician has a different theory of the operation of the four humors from his Galenic counterpart but that modern medicine has *abandoned* the four humors, and not that the Galenic physician says different things about bacteria and viruses but that he says *nothing* about them.

As long as the fundamental categories for the characterization of thought—the modes of spatiality and temporality, of structural description, functional connection, and explanatory rationalization—are not seen as necessary features of intelligence as such, but as evolved cognitive adaptations to particular contingently constituted modes of emplacement in and interaction with nature, there will be no reason to expect uniformity. Sociologists of knowledge tell us that even for us humans here on earth, our Western science is but one of many competing ways of conceptualizing the world's processes. And when one turns outward toward space at large, the prospects of diversity become virtually endless. It is a highly problematic contention even that beings constituted as we are and located in an environment such as ours must inevitably describe and explain natural phenomena in our terms. And with differently constituted beings, the basis of differentiation is amplified enormously. Our minds are the information-processing mechanisms of an organism interacting with a particular environment via certain particular senses (natural endowments, hardware) and certain culturally evolved methods (cultural endowments, software). With different sorts of beings, these resources would differ profoundly—and so would the cognitive products that would flow from their employment.

The more one reflects on the matter, the more firmly one is led to the realization that our particular human conception of the issues of science is something parochial, because we are physically, perceptually, and cognitively limited and conditioned by our specific situation within nature. Given intelligent beings with a physical and cognitive nature profoundly different from ours, one simply cannot assert with confidence what the natural science of such creatures would be like.

3. THE FLAWS OF THE ONE WORLD, ONE SCIENCE ARGUMENT

One writer on extraterrestrial intelligence poses the question, "What can we talk about with our remote friends?" and answers with the remark: "We have a lot in common. We have mathematics in common, and physics, and astronomy."[6] Another maintains that "we may fail to enjoy their music, understand their poetry, or approve their ideals; but we can talk about matters of practical and scientific concern."[7] But is it all that simple? With respect to his hypothetical Planetarians, the ingenious Christiaan Huygens wrote, three centuries ago:

> Well, but allowing these Planetarians some sort of reason, must it needs be the same with ours? Why truly I think 'tis, and must be so; whether we consider it as applied to Justice and Morality, or exercised in the Principles and Foundations of Science. . . . For the aim and design of the Creator is every where the preservation and safety of his Creatures. Now when such a reason as we are masters of, is necessary for the preservation of Life, and promoting of Society (a thing that they be not without, as we shall show) would it not be strange that the Planetarians should have such a perverse sort of Reason given them, as would necessarily destroy and confound what it was designed to maintain and defend? But allowing Morality and Passions with those Gentlemen to be somewhat different from ours, . . . yet still there would be no doubt, but that in the search after Truth, in judging of the consequences of things, in reasoning, particularly in that form which belongs to Magnitude or Quantity about which their Geometry (if they have such a thing) is employed, there would be no doubt I say, but that their Reason here must be exactly the same, and go the same way to work with ours, and that what's true in one part will hold true over the whole Universe; so that all the difference must lie in the degree of Knowledge, which will be proportional to the Genius and Capacity of the inhabitants.[8]

With the exception of a timely shift from a theological to a natural-selectionist rationale, this analysis is close to the sort of thing one hears advanced today.

It is tempting to reason: "Since there is only one nature, only one science of nature is possible." Yet, on closer scrutiny, this reasoning becomes highly problematic. Above all, it fails to reckon with the fact that while there indeed is only one world, nevertheless very different *thought-worlds* can be at issue in the elaborations of a "science."

It is surely naive to think that because one single object is in question, its description must issue in one uniform result. This view ignores the crucial impact of the describer's intellectual orientation. Minds with different concerns and interests and with different experiential backgrounds can deal with the selfsame items in ways that yield wholly disjoint and disparate result because different features of the thing are being addressed. The *things* are the same, but their significance is altogether different.

Perhaps it seems plausible to argue thus: "Common problems constrain common solutions. Intelligent alien civilizations have in common with us the problem of cognitive accommodation to a shared world. Natural science as we know it is *our* solution of this problem. Therefore, it is likely to be *theirs* as well." But this tempting argument founders on its second premise. The problem-situation confronted by extraterrestrials is *not* common with ours. Their situation must be presumed substantially different exactly because they live in a significantly different environment and come equipped with significantly different resources—physical and intellectual alike. The common problems, common solutions line does not work: to presuppose a common problem is already to beg the question.

Science is always the result of *inquiry* into nature, and this is inevitably a matter of a *transaction* or *interaction* in which nature is but one party and the inquiry beings another. We must expect alien beings to question nature in ways very different from our own. On the basis of an *interactionist* model, there is no reason to think that the sciences of different civilizations will exhibit anything more than the roughest sorts of family resemblance.

Our alien colleagues scan nature for regularities, using (at any rate, to begin with) the sensors provided to them by their evolutionary heritage. They note, record, and transmit those regularities that they find to be useful or interesting, and then develop their inquiries by theoretical triangulation from this basis. Now, this is clearly going to make for a course of development that closely gears their science to their particular situation—their biological endowment ("their sensors"), their cultural heritage ("what is pragmatically useful"). Where these key parameters differ, we must expect that the course of scientific development will differ as well.

Admittedly, there is only one universe, and its laws and materials are, as far as we can tell, the same everywhere. We share this common universe with all life forms. However radically we differ in other respects (in particular, those relating to environment, to natural endowments, and to style or civilization), we have a common background of cosmic evolution and a common heritage of natural laws. And so, if intelligent aliens investigate nature at all, they will investigate the same nature we ourselves do. All this can be agreed. But the fact remains that the corpus of scientific information—ours or anyone's—is an ideational construction. And the sameness of the object of contemplation does nothing to guarantee the sameness of ideas about it. It is all too familiar a fact that even where only human observers are at issue, very different constructions are often placed upon "the same" occurrences. As is clearly shown by the rival interpretations of different psychological schools—to say nothing of the court testimony of rival "experts" —there need be little uniformity in the conceptions held about one selfsame object from different "perspectives of consideration." The fact that all intelligent beings inhabit the same world does not countervail the no less momentous fact that we inhabit very different ecological niches within it, engendering very different sorts of modus operandi.

The universality and intersubjectivity of our science, its repeatability and investigator-independence, still leave matters at the level of *human* science. As C. S. Peirce was wont to insist, the aim of scientific inquiry is to allay *our* doubts—to resolve the sorts of questions we ourselves deem worth posing. Different sorts of beings might well ask very different sorts of questions.

No one who has observed how very differently the declarations of a single text (the Bible, say, or the dialogues of Plato) have been interpreted and understood over the centuries—even by people of a common culture heritage—can be hopeful that that study of a common object by different civilizations must be lead to a uniform result. Yet, such textual analogies are oversimple and misleading, because the scientific study of nature is not a matter of decoding a preexisting text. There just is not one fixed basic text—the changeless "book of nature writ large"—which different civilizations can decipher in different degrees. Like other books, it is to some extent a mirror: what looks out depends on who looks in.

The development of a "science"—a specific codification of the laws of nature—always requires as input some inquirer-supplied element of determination. The result of such an interaction depends crucially on the contribution from both sides—from nature and from the intelligences that interact with it. A kind of "chemistry" is at work in which nature provides only one input and the inquirers themselves provide another—one that can massively and dramatically affect the outcome in such a way that we cannot disentangle the respective contributions of nature and the inquirer. Things cannot of themselves dictate the significance that an active intelligence can attach to them. Human organisms are essentially similar, but there is not much similarity between the medicine of the ancient Hindus and that of the ancient Greeks.

After all, throughout the earlier stages of man's intellectual history, different human civilizations developed their "natural sciences" in substantially different ways. The shift to an extraterrestrial setting is bound to amplify this diversity. The "science" of an alien civilization may be far more remote from ours than the "language" of our cousin the dolphin is remote from our language. We must face, however reluctantly, the fact that on a cosmic scale the "hard" physical sciences have something of the same cultural relativity that one encounters with the "softer" social sciences on a terrestrial basis.

There is no categorical assurance that intelligent creatures will *think* alike in a common world, any more than that they will *act* alike—that is, there is no reason why *cognitive* adaptation should be any more uniform than *behavioral* adaptation. Thought, after all, is simply a kind of action; and as the action of a creature reflects its biological heritage, so does its mode of thought.

These considerations point to a clear lesson. Different civilizations composed of different sorts of creatures must be expected to create diverse "sciences." Though inhabiting the same physical universe with us, and subject to the same sorts of fundamental regularities, they must be expected to create as cognitive artifacts different depictions of nature, reflecting their different modes of emplacement within it.

Each inquiring civilization must be expected to produce its own, perhaps ever-changing, cognitive products—all more or less adequate in their own ways but with little if any actual overlap in conceptual content.

Natural science—broadly construed as inquiry into the ways of nature—is something that is in principle endlessly plastic. Its development will trace out an historical course closely geared to the specific capacities, interest, environment, and opportunities of the creatures that develop it. We are deeply mistaken if we think of it as a process that must follow a route generally parallel to ours and issue in a roughly comparable product. It would be grossly unimaginative to think that either the journey or the destination must be the same—or even substantially similar.

Factors such as capacities, requirements, interests, and course of development are bound to affect the shape and substance of the science and technology of any particular space-time region. Unless we narrow our intellectual horizons in a parochially anthropomorphic way, we must be prepared to recognize the great likelihood that the "science" and "technology" of a remote civilization would be something *very* different from science and technology as we know it. Our human sort of natural science may well be *sui generis*, adjusted to and coordinated with a being of our physical constitution, inserted into the orbit of the world's processes and history in our sort of way. It seems that in science, as in other areas of human endeavor, we are prisoners of the thought-world that our biological and social and intellectual heritage affords us.

Our science is bound to be limited in crucial respects by the very fact of it being *our* science. A tiny creature living its brief life span within a maple leaf could never recognize that such leaves are deciduous—themselves part of a cyclic process. The processes of this world of ours (even unto its utter disappearance) could make no cognitive impact upon a being in whose body our entire universe is but a single atom. No doubt the laws of our world are (part of) the laws of its world as well, but this circumstance is wholly without practical effect. Where causal processes do not move across the boundaries between worlds—where the levels of relevantly operative law are so remote that nothing happening at the one level makes any substantial impact on the other—there can be little if any overlap in "science." Science is limited to the confines of discernibility: as Kant maintained, the limits of our experience set limits to our science.

A deep question arises: Is the mission of intelligence in the cosmos uniform or diversified? Two fundamentally opposed philosophical views are possible with respect to cognitive evolution in its cosmic perspective. The one is a *monism* that sees the universal mission of intelligence in terms of a certain shared destination, the attainment of a common cosmic "position of reason as such." The other is a *pluralism* that sees each intelligent cosmic civilization as forgoing its own characteristic cognitive destiny, and takes it as the mission of intelligence as such to span a wide spectrum of alternatives and to realize a vastly diversified variety of possibilities, with each thought-form achieving its one peculiar destiny in separation from all the rest. The conflict between these doctrines must in the final analysis be settled triangulation from the empirical data. This said, it must be recognized that the whole tendency of these present deliberations is toward the pluralistic side. It seems altogether plausible to see cognition as an evolutionary product that is bound to attune its practitioners to the characteristic peculiarities of their particular niche in the world order.

4. INACCESSIBILITY

There is, no doubt, a certain charm to the idea of companionship. It would be comforting to reflect that however estranged from them we are in other ways, those alien minds share *science* with us at any rate and are our fellow travelers on a common journey of inquiry. Our yearning for companionship and contact runs deep. It might be pleasant to think of ourselves not only as colleagues but as junior collaborators whom other, wiser minds might be able to help along the way. Even as many in sixteenth-century Europe looked to those strange pure men of the Indies (East or West) who might serve as moral exemplars for sinful European man, so we are tempted to look to alien inquirers who surpass us in scientific wisdom and might assist us in overcoming our cognitive deficiencies. The idea is appealing, but it is also, alas, very unrealistic.

Life on other worlds might be very different from the life we know. It could very well be based on a multivalent element other than carbon and be geared to a medium other than water—perhaps even one that is solid or gaseous rather than liquid. In his splendid book entitled *The Immense Journey*, Loren Eiseley wrote:

> Life, even cellular life, may exist out yonder in the dark. But high or low in nature, it will not wear the shape of man. That shape is the evolutionary product of a strange, long wandering through the attics of the forest roof, and so great are the chances of failure, that nothing precisely and identically human is likely ever to come that way again.[9]

What holds for the material configuration of the human shape would seem no less applicable to the cognitive configuration of human thought. It is plausible to think that alien creatures will solve the problems of *intellectual* adjustment to their environment in ways as radically different from ours as those by which they solve the problems of physical adjustment. The physics of an alien civilization need resemble ours no more than does their physical therapy. We must be every bit as leery of *cognitive* anthropomorphism as of *structural* anthropomorphism. (Fred Hoyle's science-fiction story entitled *The Black Cloud* is thought-provoking in this regard.[10] The cloud tells a scientist what it knows about the world. The result is schizophrenia and untimely death for the scientist: the cloud's information is divergent and compelling.)

With respect to biological evolution it seems perfectly sensible to reason as follows:

> What can we say about the forms of life evolving on these other worlds? . . . [I]t is clear that subsequent evolution by natural selection would lead to an immense variety of organisms; compared to them, all organisms on Earth, from molds to men, are very close relations.[11]

The same situation will surely obtain with respect to cognitive evolution. The "sciences" produced by different civilizations here on earth—the ancient Chinese, Indians, and Greeks for example—unquestionably exhibit an infinitely greater similarity than obtains between our present-day science and anything devised by astronomically remote alien civilizations. And the concept-scheme they use in their scientific endeavors may be wholly inaccessible to us.

The point of these deliberations is straightforward. The facts about the world that are available to an intelligent creature within it will depend upon the resources at its disposal for observational experience in the nature of its embedding in the future of regularity that makes for the systemic "concern of experience" that grounds its conceptualizations. And the facts that are accessible to a given species in its contexts will not be—and cannot be expected to be—available to another.

The world's facts are a matter of interaction—of "regularities" if you will—between the modus operandi of an intelligent organism and its life-context. In this regard we cannot but expect that the facts available to one intelligent species will be identical with those of another. Undoubtedly some of the facts known to the intelligent creatures of an alien civilization—if such there are—are bound to lie outside of our cognitive reach. Their experience of the world will deliver facts about it into their possession that are bound to remain unknown to us.

REFERENCES

Note: This listing is confined to those relevant materials that I have found particularly interesting or useful. It does not aspire to comprehensiveness. A much fuller bibliography is given in MacGowan and Ordway, 1966.

Allen, Thomas Barton. *The Quest: A Report on Extraterrestrial Life*. Philadelphia: Chilton Books, 1965. (An imaginative survey of the issues.)

Anderson, Paul. *Is There Life on Other Worlds?* New York and London: Collier-Macmillan, 1963. (Chapter 8, "On the Nature and Origin of Science," affords many perceptive observations.)

Ball, John A. "Extraterrestrial Intelligence: Where Is Everybody?" *American Scientist* 68 (1980): 565–663.

———. "The Zoo Hypothesis," *Icarus* 19 (1973): 347–49. (Aliens are absent because the Intergalactic Council has designated Earth a nature reserve.)

Beck, Lewis White. "Extraterrestrial Intelligent Life." *Proceedings and Addresses of the American Philosophical Association* 45 (1971–1972): 5–21. (A thoughtful and very learned discussion.)

Berrill, N. J. *Worlds without End*. London: Macmillan, 1964. (A popular treatment.)

Bracewell, Ronald N. *The Galactic Club: Intelligent Life in Outer Space*. San Francisco: W. H. Freeman, 1975. (A lively and enthusiastic survey of the issues.)

Breuer, Reinhard. *Contact with the Stars*. Trans. by C. Payne-Gaposchkin and M. Lowery. New York: W. H. Freeman, 1982. (Maintains that we are the only technologically developed civilization in the galaxy.)

Cameron, A. G. W., ed. *Interstellar Communication: A Collection of Reprints and Original Contributions*. New York and Amsterdam: W. A. Benjamin, 1963. (A now somewhat dated but still useful collection.)

Dick, Steven J. *Plurality of Worlds: The Origins of the Extraterrestrial Life Debate from Democritus to Kant*. Cambridge: Cambridge University Press, 1982. (A lively and informative survey of the historical background.)

Dole, Stephen H. *Habitable Planets for Man*. New York: Blaisdell, 1964; 2nd ed., New York: American Elsevier, 1970. (A painstaking and sophisticated discussion.) A more popular version is S. H. Dole and Iassc Asimov. *Planets for Man*. New York: Random House, 1964.

Drake, Frank D. *Intelligent Life in Space.* New York and London: Macmillan, 1962. (A clearly written, popular account.)

Ehrensvaerd, Goesta. *Man on Another World.* Chicago and London: University of Chicago Press, 1965. (See especially chapter 10 on "Advanced Consciousness.")

Firsoff, V. A. *Life Beyond the Earth: A Study in Exobiology.* New York: Basic Books, 1963. (A detailed study of the biochemical possibilities for extraterrestrial life.)

Gavvay, Allen. "Les Principes foundamenteaus de la conaissance: Le Modele des intelligenes extraterrêtres." *Science, Histoire, Épistémologie: Actes du Premier Colloque Européen d'Histoire et Philosophie des Sciences.* Paris: J. Vrin, 1981: 33–59. (A stimulating philosophical discussion.)

Hart, M. H. "An Explanation for the Absence of Extraterrestrials on Earth." *Quarterly Journal of the Royal Astronomical Society* 16 (1975): 128–35. (A perceptive survey of this question.)

Herrmann, Joachim. *Leven auf anderen Sternen.* Guetersloh: Bertelsmann Verlag, 1963. (A thoughtful and comprehensive survey with special focus on the astronomical issues.)

von Hoerner, Sevastian. "Astronomical Aspects of Interstellar Communication." *Astronautica Acta* 18 (1973): 421–29. (A useful overview of key issues.)

Hoyle, Fred, *Of Men and Galaxies.* Seattle: University of Washington Press, 1966. (Speculations by one of the leading astrophysicists of the day.)

Huang, Su-Shu. "Life Outside the Solar System." *Scientific American* 202, 4 (April 1960): 55–63. (A useful discussion of some of the astrophysical issues.)

Huygens, Christiaan. *Cosmotheoros: The Celestial Worlds Discovered— New Conjectures Concerning the Planetary Worlds, Their Inhabitants and Productions.* London, 1698; reprinted London F. Cass & Co., 1968. (A classic from another age. Cf. Dick, 1982.)

Jeans, Sir James. "Is There Life in Other Worlds?" A 1941 Royal Institution lecture reprinted in H. Shapley et al., eds. *Readings in the Physical Sciences.* New York: Appleton-Century-Crofts, 1948: 112–17. (A stimulating analysis.)

Kaplan, S. A., ed. *Extraterrestrial Civilization: Problems of Interstellar Communication.* Jerusalem: Israel Program for Scientific Translations, 1971. (A collection of Russian scientific papers that present interesting theoretical work.)

Lem, S. *Summa Technologiae*. Krakow: Wyd. Lt., 1964. (To judge from the ample account given in Kaplan, 1971, this book contains an extremely perceptive treatment of theoretical issues regarding extraterrestrial civilization. I have not, however, been able to consult the book itself.)

MacGowan, Roger A., and Ordway, Frederick. *Intelligence in the Universe*. Englewood Cliffs, N.J.: Prentice Hall, 1966. (A careful and informative survey of a wide range of relevant issues.)

———. "On the Possibilities of the Existence of Extraterrestrial Intelligence." In F. I. Ordway, ed. *Advances in Space Science and Technology*. New York and London: Academic Press, 1962: 4:39–111.

Nozick, Robert. "R.S.V.P.—A Story." *Commentary* 53 (1972): 66–68. (Perhaps letting aliens know about us is just too dangerous.)

Pucetti, Roland. *Persons: A Study of Possible Moral Agents in the Universe*. New York: Herder and Herder, 1969. (A stimulating philosophical treatment.) But see the sharply critical review by Ernan McMullin in *Icarus* 14 (1971): 291–94.

Rood, Robert T., and Trefil, James S. *Are We Alone: The Possibility of Extraterrestrial Civilization*. New York: Scribners, 1981. (An interesting discussion of the key issues.)

Sagan, Carl. *The Cosmic Connection*. New York: Doubleday, 1973. (A well-written, popularly oriented account.)

———. *Cosmos*. New York: Random House, 1980. (A modern classic.)

Shapley, Harlow. *Of Stars and Men*. Boston: Beacon Press, 1958. (See especially the chapter entitled "An Inquiry Concerning Other Worlds.")

Shklovskii, I. S., and Sagan, Carl. *Intelligent Lifer in the Universe*. San Francisco, London, Amsterdam: Holden-Day, 1966. (A well-informed and provocative survey of the issues.)

Simpson, George Gaylord. "The Nonprevalence of Humanoids." *Science* 143 (1964): 769–75. Chapter 13 of *This View of Life: The World of an Evolutionist*. New York: Harcourt Brace, 1964. (An insightful account of the contingencies of evolutionary development by a mater of the subject.)

Sullivan, Walter. *We Are Not Alone*. New York: McGraw Hill, 1964; rev. ed., 1965. (A very well-written survey of the historical background and of the scientific issues.

NOTES

1. Compare the discussion in Gösta Ehrensvärd, *Man on Another World* (Chicago and London: University of Chicago Press, 1965), 146–148.

2. His anthropological investigations pointed Benjamin Lee Whorf in much this same direction. He wrote: "The real question is: What do different languages do, not with artificially isolated objects, but with the flowing face of nature in its motion, color, and changing form; with clouds, beaches, and yonder flight of birds? For as goes our segmentation of the face of nature, so goes our physics of the cosmos" ("Language and Logic," in *Language, Thought, and Reality*, ed. by J. B. Carroll [Cambridge, Mass.: Technology Press of Massachusetts Institute of Technology, 1956], 240–241). Compare also the interesting discussion in Thomas Nagel, "What is it Like to be a Bat?" in *Mortal Questions* (Cambridge, Mass.: Harvard University Press, 1976).

3. Thomas Kuhn, *The Structure of Scientific Revolutions* (Chicago: University of Chicago Press, 1962).

4. Georg Simmel, "Uber eine Beziehung der Kelektionslehre zur Erkenntnistheorie," *Archiv für systematische Philosophie und Soziologie* 1 (1895), 34–45. (See 40–41).

5. William James, *Pragmatism* (New York: Longmans, 1907), 171.

6. See E. Purcell in *Interstellar Communication: A Collection of Reprints and Original Contributions*, ed. by A. G. W. Cameron (New York and Amsterdam: W. A. Benjamin, 1963).

7. Paul Anderson, *Is There Life on Other Worlds?* (New York and London: Crowell-Collier Press, 1963), 130.

8. Christiaan Huygens, *Cosmotheoros: The Celestial Worlds Discovered—New Conjectures Concerning the Planetary Worlds, Their Inhabitants and Productions* (London: T. Childe, 1698), 41–43.

9. Loren Eiseley, *The Immense Journey* (New York: Random House, 1937).

10. Fred Hoyle, *The Black Cloud* (New York: Harper, 1957).

11. I. S. Shklovskii and Carl Sagan, *Intelligent Life in the Universe* (San Francisco: Holden-Day, 1966), 350.

4

Against Insolubilia

1. THE IDEA OF INSOLUBILIA

A doctrine of the incompletability in natural science because new questions emerge at every stage of its development is wholly compatible with the view that every question that can be asked at each and every particular state of natural science will be resolved at some future state. The ongoing presence of unanswered questions does not mean having ever-unanswerable ones. And in specific, it does not mean that certain questions can be identified as insolubilia—we can here and now formulate questions that can never be resolved.

The very idea that certain now-specifiable questions can be identified as never-to-be-resolved requires claiming that present science can speak for future science, that the science of today can establish what the science of tomorrow cannot do by way of dealing with the issues. And this is simply an untenable contention.

The ramifications of these issues deserve closer scrutiny.

2. THE REYMOND-HAECKEL CONTROVERSY

In the 1880s, the German physiologist, philosopher, and historian of science Emil du Bois-Reymond published a widely discussed lecture on *The Seven Riddles of the Universe* (*Die Sieben Welträtsel*).[1] In it, he maintained that some of the most fundamental problems about the workings of the world were insoluble. Reymond was a rigorous mechanist, and argued that the limit of our secure knowledge of the world is confined to the range where purely mechanical principles can be applied. Regarding anything else, we not only *do not* have but *cannot* in principle obtain reliable knowledge. Under the banner of the slogan *ignoramus et ignorabimus* ("we *do not* know and *shall never* know"), du Bois-Reymond maintained a skeptically agnostic position with respect to various foundational issues in physics (the nature of matter and force, and the ultimate source of motion) and psychology (the origin of sensation and of consciousness). These basic issues are simply explanatory *insolubilia* that altogether transcend man's scientific capabilities. Certain fundamental biological problems he regarded as unsolved but perhaps in principle soluble (though very difficult): the origin of life, the adaptiveness of organisms, and the development of language and reason. And as regards his seventh riddle—the problem of freedom of the will—he was undecided.

The position of du Bois-Reymond was soon sharply contested by the zoologist Ernest Haeckel, in a book *Die Welträtsel*, published in 1889,[2] which attained a great popularity. Far from being intractable or even insoluble—so Haeckel maintained—the riddles of du Bois-Reymond had all virtually been solved. Dismissing the problem of free will as a pseudo-problem—since free will "is a pure dogma [which] rests on mere illusion and in reality does not exist at all"—Haeckel turned with relish to the remaining riddles. Problems of the origin of life, of sensation, and of consciousness Haeckel regarded as solved—or solvable—by appeal to the theory of evolution. Questions of the nature of matter and force he regarded as solved by modern physics except for one residue: the problem (perhaps less scientific than metaphysical) of the ultimate origin of matter and its laws. This "problem of substance" was the only riddle recognized by Haeckel, but was downgraded by him as not really a problem for science. In discovering the "fundamental law of the conservation of matter and force," science had done pretty much what it could do with respect to this problem; what remained was metaphysics, with which the scientist has no proper concern. Haeckel summarized his position as follows:

> The number of world-riddles has been continually diminishing in the course of the nineteenth century through the aforesaid progress of a true knowledge of nature. Only one comprehensive riddle of the universe now remains—the problem of substance. . . . [But now] we have the great, comprehensive "law of substance," the fundamental law of the constancy of matter and force. The fact that

substance is everywhere subject to eternal movement and transformation gives it the character also of the universal law of evolution. As this supreme law has been firmly established, and all others are subordinate to it, we arrive at a conviction of the universal unity of nature and the eternal validity of its laws. From the gloomy *problem* of substance we have evolved the clear *law* of substance.[3]

The basic structure of Haeckel's position is clear: science is rapidly nearing a state in which all big problems admit of solution—substantially including those "insolubilia" of du Bois-Reymond. (What remains unresolved is not so much a *scientific* as a *metaphysical* problem.) Haeckel concluded that natural science in its *fin de siècle* condition had pretty much accomplished its mission—reaching a state in which all scientifically legitimate problems were substantially resolved.

The dispute exhibits the interesting phenomenon of a controversy in which both sides went wrong.

Du Bois-Reymond was badly wrong in claiming to have identified various substantive insolubilia. The idea that there are any identifiable issues that science cannot ever resolve has little to recommend. To be sure, various efforts along these lines have been made:

- The attempts of eighteenth-century mechanists to bar action at a distance.
- The attempts of early-twentieth-century vitalists to put life outside the range of scientific explicability.
- The attempts of modern materialists to exclude hypnotism or autosuggestion or parapsychology as spurious on grounds of scientific intractability.

But the historical record does not augur well in this regard. The annals of science are replete with achievements which, before the fact, most theoreticians had insisted could not possibly be accomplished. The course of historical experience runs counter to the idea that there are any identifiable questions about the world that do in principle lie beyond the reach of science. It is always risky to say *never*, and particularly so with respect to the prospects of knowledge. Never is a long time, and "never say never," is a more sensible motto than its paradoxical appearance might indicate.

All the same, Haeckel was no less seriously wrong in his insistence that natural science was nearing the end of the road—that the time was approaching when it would be able to provide definitive answers to the key questions of the field. The entire history of science shouts support for the conclusion that even where "answers" to our explanatory questions are attained, the prospect of revision—of fundamental changes of mind—is ever-present. For sure, Haeckel was gravely mistaken in his claim that natural science had attained a condition of effective completeness.

And yet, both these theorists were, in a way, also right. But du Bois-Reymond correctly saw that the work of science will never be completed, that science can never shut up shop in the final conviction that the job is finished. And Haeckel was surely right in denying the existence of identifiable insolubilia.

3. SOME PURPORTED SCIENTIFIC INSOLUBILIA

Consider some examples of proposed scientific insolubilia:

- Why is there anything rather than nothing? Why are there physical things at all? Why does *anything* exist?
- Why is nature an orderly cosmos? Why are there any natural laws (uniformities, regularities) at all? Why are there causal laws to operate as "the cement of the universe"?
- Granted that there are (perhaps even must be) things and laws, why are they as they are rather than otherwise? Why were the "initial conditions" thuswise, and why are the laws as they are? (For example, why are the laws so orderly rather than more chaotic?)

Notice, first of all, the global and universalistic character of these "ultimate questions" cast in the role of insolubilia. When we try to answer these questions by the usual device of explaining one thing in terms of another, the former immediately expands to swallow up the latter. The usual form of explanation (subsuming boundary conditions under laws) at once falls into question in a way that makes the explanatory process circular. This totalitarian aspect gives the whole issue a case that is more philosophical than scientific. The questions at issue relate not so much to the discoveries as to the presuppositions of science.

In theory, there are four lines of response to such "ultimate questions":

I. They are illegitimate and improper questions, based on defective presuppositions.

II. They are legitimate
   1. but unanswerable: they represent a *mystery*
   2. and answerable
      a. via a substantively causal route that centers on a substance (God)
         that is self-generated (*causa sui*) and is, in turn, the efficient causal
         source of everything else.
      b. via a nonsubstantival route that centers on some creatively hylarchic
         principle that has no basis in some preexisting thing or group
         thereof, a principle that envisions agencies without agents.

Alternative I represents a choice of last resort—one that sidesteps rather than
confronts the question. Alternative II/1 is not particularly appealing; its recourse
to mystery leaves us with the worst of both worlds. Alternative II/2a obviously
has its problems in an era where people still continue to endorse the medieval
principle that *in philosophia non recurre est and deum* (roughly: "Don't call on
God to pull your philosophical chestnuts out of the fire"). And so, considering
that all of the other alternatives are unpromising and problematic, II/2b deserves
consideration. The idea of a creative principle is at least worth entertaining.

It is instructive to consider more closely some of the issues raised by these
three "insoluble" problems, focusing on that seemingly most intractable issue:
"Why is there anything at all?"

Dismissal of this problem as illegitimate is generally based on the idea that
it involves an illicit presupposition. It looks to answers of the form "Z is the
(or *an*) explanation for the existence of things." In standing committed to this
response-schema, the question presupposes the thesis "There is a ground for
the existence of things; existence in general is the sort of thing that has an explanation." And this presumption—we are told—is or may well be false.

In principle, this presumed falsity could emerge in two ways:

1. on grounds of deep general principle inherent in the conceptual "logic" of
   the situation; or
2. on grounds of a concrete doctrine of substantive metaphysics or science that
   precludes the prospect of an answer—even as quantum theory precludes the

prospect of an answer to "Why did that atom of californium decay at that particular time?"

Now as regards the first alternative, the question of the world's existence might well be invalidated by considerations of the first sort deep-rooted in the conceptual nature of things. Consider the following contention by C. G. Hempel:

> Why is there anything at all, rather than nothing? . . . But what kind of an answer could be appropriate? What seems to be wanted is an explanatory account which does not assume the existence of something or other. But such an account, I would submit, is a logical impossibility. For generally, the question "Why is it the case that A? is answered by "Because B is the case.". . . [A]n answer to our riddle which made no assumptions about the existence of anything cannot possibly provide adequate grounds. . . . The riddle has been constructed in a manner that makes an answer logically impossible. . . .[4]

However, this plausible problem-rejecting line of argumentation is not without its shortcomings. The most serious of these is that it fails to distinguish appropriately between the *existence of things*, on the one hand, and the *obtaining of facts*, on the other,[5] and supplementarily also between specifically substantival facts regarding existing things, and nonsubstantival facts regarding *states of affairs* that are not dependent on the operation of preexisting things.

We are confronted here with a principle of hypostatization to the effect that the reason for anything must ultimately always inhere in the operations of things. And at this point we come to a prejudgment or prejudice as deep-rooted as any in Western philosophy: the idea that things can only originate from things, that nothing can come from nothing (*ex nihilos nihil fit*), in the sense that no thing can emerge from a thingless condition. Now, this somewhat ambiguous principle is perfectly unproblematic when construed as saying that if the existence of something real has a correct explanation at all, then this explanation must pivot on something that is really and truly so. Clearly, we cannot explain one fact without involving other *facts* to do the explaining. But the principle becomes highly problematic when construed in the manner of the precept that "*things* must come from *things*," that *substances* must inevitably be invoked to explain the existence of *substances*. For we then become committed to the thesis that everything in nature has an efficient cause in some other natural thing that is somehow its causal source, its reason for being.

This stance lies at the basis of Hempel's argument. And it is explicit in much of the philosophical tradition. Hume, for one, insists that there is no feasible way in which an existential conclusion can be obtained from nonexistential premises.[6] And the principle is also supported by philosophers of a very different ilk on the other side of the channel—including Leibniz himself, who writes: "The sufficient reason [of contingent existence] . . . must be outside this series of contingent things, and *must reside in a substance which is the cause of this series.* . . ."[7] Such a view amounts to a thesis of genetic homogeneity which says (on analogy with the old but now rather obsolete principle that "life must come from life") that "things must come from things," or "stuff must come from stuff," or "substance must come from substance."

Is it indeed true that only *things* can engender things? Must substance inevitably arise from *substance*? Even to state such a principle is in effect to challenge its credentials. And this challenge is not easily met. Why must the explanation of facts rest in the operation of *things*? To be sure, fact-explanations must have inputs (*all* explanations must). Facts must root in facts. But why thing-existential ones? To pose these questions is to recognize that a highly problematic bit of metaphysics is involved here. Dogmas about explanatory homogeneity aside, there is no discernible reason why an existential fact cannot be grounded in nonexistential ones, and why the existence of substantial *things* cannot be explained on the basis of some nonsubstantival circumstance or principle whose operations can constrain existence in something of the way in which equations can constrain nonzero solutions. Once we give up this principle of genetic homogeneity and abandon the idea that existing things must originate in existing things, we remove the key prop of the idea that asking for an explanation of things in general is a logically inappropriate demand. The footing of the rejectionist approach is gravely undermined.

After all, rejectionism is not a particularly appealing course. Any alternative to rejectionism has the significant merit of retaining for rational inquiry and investigation a question that would otherwise be intractable. The question of "the reason why" behind existence is surely important. If there is any possibility of getting an adequate answer—by hook or by crook—it seems reasonable that we would very much like to have it. There is nothing patently meaningless about this "riddle of existence." And it does not seem to rest in any obvious way

Table 4.1.   An Inconsistent Quartet

1. Everything in nature (macroscopic) has a causal explanation. [The Principle of Causality]
2. Natural existence as a whole must itself be counted as a natural thing: the universe itself qualifies as a substance—a thing. [The Principle of Aggregative Homogeneity: The universe consists of things (substances) and is itself a thing (substance).]
   A. The universe has a causal explanation. [From (1) and (2)]
3. Causal explanation of existential facts requires existential inputs to afford the requisite causes. [The Principle of Genetic Homogeneity]
4. No existential inputs are available to explain the existence of natural existence as a whole, the totality of things within the world (= the universe). For any existence involved by the explanation would constitute part of the explanatory problem, thus vitiating the explanation on grounds of circularity. [The Principle of Causal Comprehension: Anything that stands in causally explanatory connection with the universe is thereby, ipso facto, a part of it.]
5. No (adequate) causal explanation can be given for the universe. [From (3) and (4)]

on any particularly problematic presupposition—apart from the epistemically optimistic idea that there are always reasons why things are as they are (the "principle of sufficient reason"). To dismiss the question as improper and illegitimate is fruitless. Try as we will to put the question away, it comes back to haunt us.[8]

Consider in this light the line of reasoning set out in table 4.1. Since assertions (1) and (5) squarely contradict each other, it is clear that theses (1)–(4) constitute an inconsistent group of propositions. One of this quartet, at least, must be rejected.

Let us explore the options for resolving this inconsistency:

(1) —*rejection.* One could abandon the Principle of Causality. This would pave the way for accepting the universe (natural science as a whole) as an item whose existence is uncaused. For obvious reasons, this is not a particularly attractive option.

(2) —*rejection.* One could abandon The Principle of Aggregative Homogeneity and maintain that the assimilation of the universe itself to particular things must be abandoned. Everything as a whole is seen as *sui generis* and thus not as a literal *thing* that, along with particular things, can be expected to conform to the Principle of Causality. Accordingly, we would exempt the universe itself from membership in the class of things that have cause. The difficulty with this approach lies in the problem of establishing the grounds of the purported impropriety. We unhesitatingly view

galaxies as individual things whose origin, endurance, and nature need explanation. Why not, then, the cosmos as a whole?

(3) —*rejection.* One could reject (3), as we have in fact already proposed to do. Yet in dismissing genetic homogeneity, one would (and should) not abandon it altogether but rather subject it to a distinction. One could then say that there are *two different kinds* of causal explanations: those that proceed in terms of the causal agency of *things* (substance causality, or S-causality for short), and those that proceed in terms of the causal operation of *principles* (P-causality). Unlike substance causality (S-causality), P-causality would not require that the causal principle at issue be rooted in the operations of "things." In its preparedness to let laws rather than things exert causal efficacy, the hylarchic principle it envisages would not presuppose any specifically substantival embodiment whatsoever. Such an approach abandons the deep-rooted prejudice that causal agency must always be hypostatized as the operation of a causal agent. This option envisages a mode of "causality" whose operation can dispense with existential inputs. It recognizes that the orthodox terms of ordinary efficient causality are not the only ones available for developing explanations of existence. Thus, while still retaining the Principle of Causality as per (1), this approach substantially alters its import.

(4) —*rejection.* This course commits us to the idea that existential inputs are available to explain the existence of natural existence as a whole. Standardly, this involves the invocation of a nature-external, literally supernatural being (God) to serve as the once-and-for-all existential ground in explaining the existence of all natural things. On this *theological* alternative, one would then retain (1) intact by means of the principle that God is *causa sui.* We have already remarked on the methodological shortcomings of this approach. A rational division of labor calls for leaving God to theology and refraining from drafting him into service in the project of scientific explanation.

It must be recognized that each of these solutions exacts a price. Each calls on us to abandon a thesis that has substantial *prima facie* plausibility and appeal. And each requires us to tell a fairly complicated and in some degree unpalatable story to excuse (that is, to explain and justify) the abandonment at issue.

The point to be emphasized, however, is that (3)—rejection—the recourse, in existence explanation, to a principle that does not itself have an existential grounding in a thing of some sort—emerges as *comparatively* optimal. The price it exacts, though real, is less than that of its competitors. The consequences it engenders are, relatively considered, on balance the least problematic—which is, of course, far from saying that they are not problematic at all. In the last analysis, we take recourse to a causality of principles—to the creative operation of principles—*faute de mieux*, because this is the contextually optimal alternative; no better one is in sight. Accordingly, the idea of a hylarchic principle that grounds the existence of things not in preexisting things but rather in a functional principle of some sort—a specifically nonsubstantival state of affairs—becomes something one can at least entertain.

But what could such a hylarchic principle be like?

What is perhaps the most promising prospect takes the form of a teleological "principle of value" to the effect that things exist because "that's for the best."[9] Such a teleological approach would hold that *being* roots in value. To be sure, this leaves a residual issue: "But why should what is fitting exist?" And here one must resist any temptation to say, "What is fitting exists because there is something [God, Cosmic Mind, and so on] that brings what is fitting to realization." This simply falls back into the causal trap. We shall have to answer the question simply in its own terms: "Because that's fitting." Fitness is seen as the end of the line.

To the objection that such an explanation strategy is inherently unscientific, one must coolly reply: "Do tell! From what mountain did your theoreticians' Moses descend with the tablets that say just what sorts of explanatory mechanisms are or are not scientific?" The scientists of the seventeenth century thought gravitational action at a distance absurd. The fashion of the present day could turn out to be just as wrong with respect to teleological explanation. We cannot put anything securely beyond the pale, because we cannot securely say where the "boundaries of science" are to be located. As we have seen, the science of one time is never in a position to speak for its successors.

This perspective has important implications. It constrains us to recognize that these purportedly intractable questions are "insoluble" not as such but merely *within the orthodox causal framework*. If we take resort to "higher ground" by expanding or supplementing or replacing this framework, such questions may well become answerable. The fact that the question "Why is there anything at all?" is indeed ultimate for the *framework of efficient causality*—which, given its own nature, cannot come to grips with the issue—does not mean that there may not be some other framework (such as the teleological framework of final causality) that can deal with this issue more or less successfully.[10] Framework-internal ultimacy will not render a question insoluble as such. Such issues bear upon the subsector-internal limitations rather than the more fundamental issue of "limits of knowledge." They represent neither unanswerable insolubilia nor "improper questions."

The problem of why the initial conditions for the universe are as they are affords yet another candidate insolubile. Some theoreticians regard this issue as lying beyond the reach of scientific explicability. W. Stanley Jevons, for example, has written as follows:

> [Darwin] proves in the most beautiful manner that each flower of an orchid is adapted to some insect which frequents and fertilises it, and these adaptations are but a few cases of those immensely numerous ones which have occurred in the lives of plants and animals. But why orchids should have been formed so differently from other plants, why anything, indeed, should be as it is, rather than in some of the other infinitely numerous possible modes of existence, he can never show. The origin of everything that exists is wrapped up in the past history of the universe. At some one or more points in past time there must have been arbitrary determinations which led to the production of things as they are.[11]

In natural science, so we are told, all we do is to make relational assertions of the form that "things are thus at *t* because they are so at *t*," and we are confined to operating on the principles of conditionality to the effect that this is so because that is so. Accordingly, to "explain" the initial conditions of natural processes—the "ultimate origins" of things—in terms of other states of the system, we would have to move to *later* times, and this would be unscientific. They have to be viewed as ultimate surds, as "arbitrary determinations" lying beyond the reach of explicability.[12]

But again the question must be pressed: Just why is a move to ex post facto explanation inherently unscientific? What is to preclude an explanatory rationalization of prior states in terms of the posteriors to which they lead? Who can legislate a priori just where science may and may not legitimately go—just what explanatory principles it may and may not use? It may well transpire that the increasingly fashionable Anthropic Principle to the general effect that "the initial conditions are as they are because otherwise intelligent life could not have evolved in the universe" involves various errors. But being inherently unscientific is not one of them.[13]

The question "Why are there any laws at all?" is seemingly less pressing than its thing-oriented cousin. After all, laws are an expression of order, and *any* order (even an emptiness or a chaos) is an order of some specifiable kind. (Even "disorder" is an order of sorts.) But of course the real question is, "Why are the laws as they are?"—that is, relatively simple, discoverable by creatures of our sort, and so on. To rationalize *such* lawfulness, one must make the transition to the level of the fundamental structure of the system of nature as a whole.

We thus arrive at that other "ultimate question" of why the overall systemic structure of nature is as it is—so orderly, simple, intelligible. In the final analysis, this question comes down to: Why is the whole systemic order of things and laws as it is rather than otherwise? And this leads us back toward the causal difficulties noted above. We cannot give a subsumptive (law-based) explanation here: laws cannot yield unproblematic support to a structure of which they themselves are part. We must again appeal outside the range of natural law and fact to those creative principles that underlay the entire existential order of nature. We arrive once more at the need for principles of a different order—for example, the teleological: they're the way they are because "that's for the best."

To be sure, the question would now arise: "How can such a teleological principle itself be explained—why should optimality exert an existential impetus?" The principle itself affords the materials needed for a response. Why should nature be optimistic? Because that, too, is for the best. The approach is smoothly self-substantiating—perfectly able to provide an explanation on its own terms, as any holistically systemic explanation would in principle have to do.

And so the route to insolubilia via "ultimate questions" can always be blocked. Since ultimacy is never absolute but framework-internal, we can defeat it by shifting to a variant explanatory framework. We must thus recognize these various purported insolubilia for what they are: not really insoluble questions whose resolution lies beyond the explanatory reach of science as such but merely questions whose natural response must be of a sort not particularly congenial to the explanatory preconceptions and prejudices of the day.

Having travelled this long road, we arrive at our desired destination. There is no need to see any of those "ultimate questions" as inherently unanswerable, provided that one is prepared to take some fairly radical steps in pushing the explanatory project beyond its more usual narrower bounds. The question at issue need not be seen as intractable insolubilia by those prepared to enclose the— surely not implausible—idea that unusual questions require unusual answers.

After all, while two "answers" may be unorthodox and eccentric the same holds for the problems they are intended to resolve.

4. THE ISSUE OF UNKNOWABLE FACT

While there undoubtedly are unanswerable questions regarding matters of world-descriptive fact, we really cannot expect to be able to identify any of them in specific. In particular, while no question within the sphere of science lies in principle beyond its resolution. By all available inclinations there are no identifiable scientific insolubilia. The quest for scientific insolubilia is a delusion; no one can say in advance just what questions natural science can and cannot answer. Identifiable insolubilia have no place in an adequate theory of scientific inquiry.

However, it deserves being noted that even if (per impossible) there were identifiable scientific insolubilia, this would not ensure the existence of identifiable unknowns. For suppose Q to be an unanswerable question—and for the sake of simplicity let it be a yes or no question. Note that even once we have *identified* Q we know that either

Q has an affirmative answer

or

Q has a negative answer

must be a fact. We have thus *localized* the fact of the matter, but we have not *identified* it. Q's hypothetical identification will not—thanks to its hypothetical unresolvability—confront us with an indefinably unknowable fact.

In the end, while the cognitive range of finite beings is indeed limited, it is also boundless. For it is not limited in a way that blocks the prospect of cognitive access to ever new and continually different facts, thereby affording an ever ampler and ever more accurate account of reality.

NOTES

1. The work was published together with a famous prior (1872) lecture on the limits of scientific knowledge as *Über die Grenzen des Naturekennens: Die Sieben Welträtsel—Zwei Vorträge*, 11th ed. (Leipzig: Veit & Co., 1916). The earlier lecture has appeared in English translation as "The Limits of Our Knowledge of Nature," *Popular Science Monthly* 5 (1874): 17–32. For du Bois-Reymond, see Ernst Cassirer, *Determinism and Indeterminism in Modern Physics: Historical and Systematic Studies of the Problem of Causality* (New Haven: Yale University Press, 1956), part I.

2. Bonn, 1889, trans. by J. McCabe as *The Riddle of the Universe—at the close of the Nineteenth Century* (New York and London: Harper & Bros., 1901). On Haeckel, see the article by Rollo Handy in *The Encyclopedia of Philosophy*, ed. by Paul Edwards, vol. III (New York: Macmillan, 1967).

3. Haeckel, *Die Welträtsel*, 365–66.

4. Carl G. Hempel, "Science Unlimited," *Annals of the Japan Association for Philosophy of Science* 14 (1973): 200 (italics added).

5. Note, too, that the question of the existence of facts is a horse of a very different color from that of the existence of things. There being no things is undoubtedly a possible situation; there being no *facts* is not (since if the situation were realized, this would itself constitute a fact).

6. N. K. Smith, ed., *Dialogues Concerning Natural Religion* (London, 1920), 189.

7. G. W. Leibniz, "Principles de la nature et de la grace," sect. 8 (italics added).

8. For criticisms of ways of avoiding the question "Why is there something rather than nothing?" see chapter 3 of William Rowe, *The Cosmological Argument* (Princeton: Princeton University Press, 1975).

9. This has been argued in detail by the Canadian philosopher John Leslie. See his paper in "The World's Necessary Existence," *International Journal for the Philosophy of Religion* 11 (1980): 297–329; "Efforts to Explain All Existence," *Mind* 87 (1978): 181–97; "The Theory that the World Exists Because It Should," *American Philosophical Quarterly* 7 (1910): 286–98; and "Anthropic Principle, World Ensemble, Design," *American Philosophical Quarterly* 19 (1982): 141–51; as well as his book *Value and Existence* (Totowa, N.J.: Rowman & Littlefield, 1979).

10. For an interesting attempt to deal with the question, see chapter 2 of Robert Nozick, *Philosophical Explanations* (Cambridge, Mass.: Harvard University Press, 1981).

11. W. Stanley Jevons, *The Principles of Science*, 2nd ed. (London: Macmillan, 1874), 764.

12. This issue is the second of du Bois-Reymond's seven "riddles of the universe."

13. For the anthropic principle, see George Gale in *Scientific American* 245 (December 1981): 154–71. See also the literature cited in Leslie's papers cited in note 9, above.

5

More Facts Than Truths

1. TRUTHS ARE ENUMERABLE

When one construes the idea of an "alphabet" sufficiently broadly to include not only letters but symbols of various sorts, it transpires that any expression that can be formulated—and thus any contention that is stateable in a language—can be spelled out in print through the concatenation of some finite register of symbols.[1] And with a "language" construed as calling for exfoliative development in the usual recursive manner, it ensues that the statements of a language can be enumerated in a vast listing—one that is a doubtless infinite but nevertheless ultimately countable listing. Moreover, since the languages that emerge in a cosmos whose past history is spatiotemporally finite will, even if not finite in number, nevertheless be at most enumerable, it follows that the set of all statements—including every linguistically formulable proposition to the effect that something or other is so—will be at most enumerably infinite.

And so, as a matter of principle we will have:

The Enumerability of Statements. Statements (linguistically formulated propositions) are in principle enumerable and thus (at most) denumerably infinite.

And therefore since *truths* (unlike *facts*) are indissolubly bound to textuality—and thereby correspond to statements—it follows that truths cannot be more than countably infinite. And on this basis we have:

> *The Denumerability of Truth.* Even though the manifold of truth cannot be finitely inventoried, nevertheless, truths, being statable, are no more than denumerably infinite in number.

"But surely there is something awry here"; it might be objected, "Surely this linguistic view of truths is untenable because even if there were no languages—if the universe had evolved without intelligent creatures—then there would still be truths." Well . . . yes and no. For one thing, truths as such would actually not vanish, since we ourselves, who deliberate not *in* but *about* that de-populated world, would still figure upon the scene. Moreover, there would certainly still be facts which, if (hypothetically) claimed as such in language, would lead to truth. But truths proper—along with claims, statements, and analogous verbalizations—would no longer be there, seeing that all this sort of thing is inherently language-correlative.

So much, then, for *truths.* But what about *facts?*

2. THE TRANSDENUMERABILITY OF FACTS

It serves the interests of clarity to draw an important distinction at this stage, that between truths and facts. Truths are linguistically formulated facts, correct statements, which, as such, must be stated in language (broadly understood to include symbol systems of various sorts). A "truth" is something that has to be framed in *linguistic/symbolic* terms—the representation of a fact through its statement in some language, so that any correct statement formulates a truth.

Facts, on the other hand, move beyond this language-bound level. For a "fact" is not a linguistic item at all, but an actual aspect of the world's state of affairs. A fact is thus a facet or feature of reality.[2] Facts correspond to *potential* truths whose actualization as such waits upon their appropriate linguistic embodiment. Truths are statements and thereby language-bound, but facts are truth-makers that outrun linguistic limits. Once duly formulated in some language, a fact yields a truth, but with facts at large there need in principle be no linguistic route to get from here to there.

After all, reality, so we must suppose, is inexhaustibly complex. Its *detail* (as Leibniz was wont to call it) is bottomless. Thus while statements in general, and therefore true statements in particular, can be enumerated, so that truths are denumerable in number—there is no reason to suppose that the same will hold for facts. On the contrary, there is every reason to think that, reality being what it is, there will be an uncountably vast manifold of facts.

And so we also arrive at:

The Inexhaustibility of Fact. Facts are infinite in number. The domain of fact is inexhaustible: there is no limit to facts about the real.

We have come to what is, in effect, the metaphysical insight that that range of fact about anything real is effectively inexhaustible. There is, as best we can tell, no limit to the world's ever-increasing complexity that comes to view with our ever-increasing technologically mediated grasp of its detail. And this means that any attempt to register fact as a whole will founder: the list is bound to be incomplete because there are facts about the list as a whole which no single entry can encompass. (There will always be a fact about any set of facts that is not a member of that set itself.)

We thus arrive at yet another principal thesis of these deliberations: Facts being too numerous for enumerabilty: *There are quantitatively more facts than truths.*

The reality of it is that the domain of fact is ampler than that of truth so that language cannot capture the entirety of fact. We live in a world that is not digital but analog and so the manifold of its states of affairs is simply too rich to be fully comprehended by our linguistically digital means.[3] The domain of fact inevitably transcends the limits of our capacity to *express* it, and a fortiori those of our capacity to canvass it in overt detail. Truth is to fact what moving pictures are to reality—a merely discretized approximation.

With regard to language too we confront a musical chairs situation. Conceivably, language at large might, in the abstract, manage to encompass non-denumerably many instances—particularly so if we indulge the prospect of idealization and resort to Bolzano's *Saetze an sich*, Frege's *denkerlose Gedanken*, and the like. But given the granular structure of a universe pervaded by atoms and molecules, only a denumerable number of language-using creatures can ever be squeezed into the fabric of the cosmos. And so the realistically practicable possibilities for fact formulation in *available* languages are at best denumerable.

But even though there may be no inherently unstatable or unknowable facts, nevertheless when reality and language play their game of musical chairs, some facts are bound to be left in the lurch when the music of language stops.

3. ARGUMENTS FOR FACT NONDENUMERABILITY

The manifold of fact is transdenumerably infinite. This can be shown by adapting an argument due to Patrick Grim,[4] which can be framed essentially as follows. The domain of fact is too vast not only for enumerability but even for contemplatability as an authentic *set* of any sort. For suppose:

(1) The totality of facts from a well-defined set F.
(2) We know from Georg Cantor's work that the cardinality of the power set (P) of F—the set of all its subsets—is greater than that of F:

$$\text{card } (F) < \text{card } P(F)$$

(3) But every member of $P(F)$ also corresponds to some unique member of F (for example, that it is the only $P(F)$ member that is identical with the one that it happened to be). Accordingly, the cardinality of $P(F)$ cannot be greater than that of F:

$$\text{card } (F) \geq \text{card } P(F)$$

The contradiction at work here constitutes a reductio ad absurdum of (1). The totality of facts does not constitute a well-defined set—it is, in effect, a manifold so vast as to preclude comprehension within the conceptual resources of standard set theory. And this consideration also puts it beyond the reach of language-formulatable truth.[5]

And other routes to the same destination are also available.

The idea of a complete listing of all the facts is manifestly impracticable. For consider the following statement. "*The list F of stated facts fails to have this statement on it.*" But now suppose this statement to be on the list. Then it clearly does not state a fact, so that the list is after all not a list of the facts (contrary to hypothesis). And so it must be left off the list. But then in consequence that list will not be complete since the statement is true. And so the nondenumerability of facts follows by considering that they can never be listed in toto because there will always be further facts—facts about the entire list itself— that a supposedly complete list could not manage to register.

This conclusion can be also argued via the following considerations. Suppose that a certain:

$$F: f_1, f_2, f_3, \ldots$$

were to constitute a *complete* enumeration of all facts. And now consider the statement:

(Z)   the list F of the form $f_1, f_2, f_3, \ldots$ is an all-inclusive listing of facts.

By hypothesis, this statement will present a fact. So if F is indeed a complete listing of *all* facts, then there will be an integer k such that:

$$Z = f_k$$

Accordingly, Z itself will occupy the k-the place on the F listing, so that:

$$f_k = \text{the list } L \text{ takes the form } f_1, f_2, f_3, \ldots f_k, \ldots$$

But this would require f_k to be an expanded version of itself, which is absurd. With the k-th position of the F listing *already* occupied by f_k we cannot also squeeze that complex f_k-involving thesis into it.

The point here is that any supposedly complete listing of facts

$$f_1, f_2, f_3 \ldots$$

will itself exhibit, as a whole, certain features that none of its individual members can encompass. Once those individual entries are fixed and the series is defined, there will be further facts about that series as a whole that its members themselves cannot articulate.

Finally, the transdenumerability of fact can also be made via an analogue of the diagonal argument that is standardly used to show that no list of real numbers can manage to include all of them, thereby establishing the transdenumerability of the reals. Let us begin by imagining a supposedly complete inventory of *independent* facts, using logic to streamline the purportedly complete listing into a condition of greater informative tidiness through the elimination of inferential redundancies so that every item adds some information to what has gone before. The argument for the transdenumerability of fact can now be developed as follows. Let us suppose (for the sake of reductio ad absurdum argumentation) that the inventory

$$f_1, f_2, f_3, \ldots$$

represents our (nonredundant but yet purportedly *complete*) listing of facts. Then by the supposition of *factuality* we have $(i)fi$. And further by the supposition of *completeness* we have it that:

$$(\forall)(p \to (\exists)[fi \to p])$$

Moreover, by the aforementioned supposition of *nonredundancy*, each member of the sequence adds something quite new to what has gone before.

$$(\forall)(\forall)[i < j \to \sim[(f1 \& f2 \& \ldots \& fi) \to fj)]]$$

Consider now the following course of reasoning.

(1) $(\forall i)fi$ by "factuality"
(2) $(\forall j)f_j \to (\exists i)(f_i \to (\forall j)f_j)$ from (1) by "completeness" via the substitution of $(\forall j)f_j$ for p
(3) $(\exists i)(f_i \to (\forall) fj)$ from (1), (2)

But (3) contradicts nonredundancy. This reductio ad absurdum of our hypothesis indicates that the facts about any sufficiently complex object will necessarily be too numerous for complete enumeration. In such circumstances, no purportedly comprehensive listing of truths can actually manage to encompass all facts because any such listing will itself bring more facts into being.

5. A SURFEIT OF FACTS

In the end, it would seem to be only right to award realism the palm of victory in its contest with nominalism. For the long and short of it is that the domain of reality-characterizing fact inevitably transcends any capacity of expressing it in language. In the description of concrete reality we are caught up in a quicksand of inexhaustible detail: There are always bound to be more descriptive facts about the world's real things than we are able to capture explicitly with our linguistic machinery. For the limitedness of our recursively constituted linguistic resources means that our characterizations of the real will always fall short owing to endless refinement and diversification of its detail.

6. SURDITY

This discrepancy between factual reality and cognized truth is perhaps not as ominous as first thought suggests. For one can distinguish between two very different modes of reference, namely specific *mention* and generic *allusion.* The situation at issue pivots on the distinction between *particular* facts that truths specifically and directly identify as such, and the *generic* and group-collectivized facts to which one merely alludes generally and indirectly via generalities.

And so, granted, given the recursive nature of symbolism, only a denumerable number of reals can ever be specifically identified and individually considered. But nevertheless the limited resources at our disposal leave open the prospect of discussing the transfinite vastness of reals at large. We can indeed obtain cognitive access here—but only at the level of abstract generality. For no recursively articulated set of truths can encompass the entire manifold of detailed fact.

Still, notwithstanding the limited resources at our disposal for dealing with the transfinite vastness of reals at large, we can in fact perhaps secure adequate access here—albeit only at the level of departicularized group-correlative schematic generalizations.

However, yet another instructive consideration comes into play. A fact is *surd* if it cannot be explained on the basis of general principles—in effect, if it cannot be derived from the definitions and laws of its natural domain. Most of the biographical facts about human individuals are surd: no matter how you identify someone ("the eldest son of X and Y"; "the man who shot Lincoln", etc.) most of the facts regarding this person cannot possibly be substantiated from generalities that obtain for homo sapiens at large. Again, while the rules of chess and the defining specifications of the pieces will very much restrict how games are played, nevertheless the actual unfolding of any given game will remain surd: they depend upon the decisions of the players and are not necessitated by reasoning from the situation at hand via the operative generalities. And in general, various facts about concrete particulars will ever elude anyone who is able only to look at things through the eyeglass of generality. For with the factual matters within the fabric of the world's contingency as woven by choice and chance there is bound to be a plethora of surd facts.

7. THE ROLE OF NUMERICAL DISPARITY IN VALIDATING CLAIMS OF INAPPLICABILITY: THE MUSICAL CHAIRS PERPLEX

What might be called the "Musical Chair Principle" plays a key role in the context of unknowability. For consider the game of that name. Here there will here be no player who is inherently unseatable: *individually* considered *any* player could be seated. But matters stand otherwise *collectively*. It is not possible—indeed impossible as a matter of necessity—that *every* player can be seated. While seatability is distributively universal among the individuals involved, the collective inevitability of unseated individuals is inescapable. While any one of the players *can* be seated, some must remain unseated. And much the same situation obtains in the context of the present deliberations regarding our knowledge of facts.

Consider an illustration of this sort of situation. There are infinitely many positive integers. But our planet has a beginning and end in time. Its overall history has room for only a finite number of intelligent earthlings, each of whom can only make specific mention of a finite number of integers within their finite lifespan. (They can, of course, refer to the set of integers at large via generalizations, but they can only take note of a finite number of them individually and specifically.) As far as we humans are concerned, there will accordingly be some ever-unmentioned, ever-unconsidered integers—indeed an infinite number of them. But clearly no one among us can give a specific example of this. So while there are bound to be (infinitely many) ever-unmentioned integers (and ever-uncognized individual facts about them), we nevertheless cannot possibly provide even a single example of this.

Or take yet another illustration. The inevitability of unproven facts in any axiomatic system of real-number arithmetic has been clear ever since the work of Georg Cantor in the nineteenth century. For consider:

- The recursive nature of axiomatization means that the totality of theorems that can possibly be proven in any formal axiomatized system of real-number arithmetic is denumerable.
- There are trans-denumberably many real numbers.
- Every real number has a characteristic identity, so that there is always some fact that holds for it alone. Accordingly, there are at least as many distinct arithmetical facts in this field as there are real numbers.

This situation of disparity obviously means that the totality of facts in real-number arithmetic can never be completely axiomatized in a way that fits out *every* fact with an explicit proof. (To be sure, *any* specified fact within a given domain is in principle demonstrable—that is, derivable from its axioms. For if it happens to be independent of the axioms at hand, it itself could always be adjoined to those axioms to obtain an enlarged and "improved" axiomatization of the field.

Now the situation about facts is going to be much like this. Possibly—perhaps even probably—no identifiable fact is going to be unknowable. Yet, nevertheless, some facts are bound to remain ever-unknown.

And no matter how we twist or tune, there are always going to be unknowable facts—notwithstanding their unidentifiability.

8. THE UNKNOWABLE MEGAFACT

The numerical discrepancy at issue with the Musical Chairs Perplex with regard to facts does no more than to demonstrate the existence of *unknown* facts, without going so far as to establish the existence of facts that are inherently *unknowable* and cannot, as a matter of principle, possibly be known. There clearly is, however, one fact that is unstatable in language and thereby unknowable by creatures whose factual knowledge is confined to the linguistically formulatable. This is the grand megafact consisting of the amalgamation of all facts whatsoever. For facts will always concatenate into further facts—even if there is an infinitude of them.

An important point emerges here. With musical chairs the totality of individuals does not combine to form a single unseatable mega-individual. But the totality of facts—all of which cannot possibly be known—does indeed combine to form one grand unknowable megafact.

But this is not so with truths. As linguistic objects they will always be finite in scope. For language-dependent knowers can at most and at best have cognitive access to a denumerable number of facts, whereas factricity itself in principle encompasses a nondenumerable quantity. And since facts can only be identified by stating truths, their range is bound to outrun our reach.

So here indeed we have managed to individuate a particular unknowable fact, namely that all-encompassing megafact. But of course while we know *that* it is unknowable, we do not know *what* it is. We have *individuated* but not *identified* it. So here, as elsewhere, the details of our ignorance are hidden from our sight.

NOTES

1. Compare Philip Hugly and Charles Sayward, "Can a Language Have Indenumerably Many Expressions?" *History and Philosophy of Logic*, vol. 4, 1983.

2. Our position thus takes no issue with P. F. Strawson's precept that "facts are what statements (when true) state." ("Truth," *Proceedings of the Aristotelian Society*, Supplementary 24 (1950): 129–56; see 136.) Difficulty would ensue with Strawson's thesis only if an "only" were added.

3. Wittgenstein writes "logic is not a body of doctrine, but a mirror-image of the world" (*Tractatus*, 6.13). This surely gets it wrong: logic is one instrumentality (among others) for organizing our thought about the world, and this thought is (at best and at most) a venture in *describing* or *conceiving* the world and its modus operandi in a way that—life being what it is—will inevitably be imperfect, and incomplete. And so any talk of mirroring is a totally unrealistic exaggeration here.

4. Patrick Grim, "There is No Set of All Truths," *Analysis* 44 (1984): 206–8.

5. The preceding argumentation turns on the fact that while *every* subset of *F* (infinite subsets included) will be a member of *P(F)*, nevertheless not every such subset will analogously engender an *F* member. Thus we cannot conjoin infinitely many sentences into yet another sentence nor infinitely many stories into yet another story, seeing that sentences and stories must be of finite scope. But an infinite complex of facts is still a fact and an infinite agglomeration of items yet another item. On this basis it transpires that while sentences and stories will constitute sets, the manifold of facts and of items (things, objects) is outsize and represents something outside the range of sets as generally conceived on logico-mathematical principles.

On Predicate Vagrancy and Its Epistemic Basis

1. VAGRANT PREDICATES AND THEIR NONINSTANTIABILITY

In addressing the idea of insuperable limits to knowledge, it is instructive to note that one can refer to an item in two distinctly different ways: either specifically and individually through a naming or identifying characterization ("George Washington," or "the Father of our Country"), or merely obliquely and sortally as an item of a certain type or kind ("an American general born in the 18th century"). Now an important albeit eccentric mode of reference occurs when an item is referred to obliquely in such a way that, as a matter of principle, any and all prospect of its specific identification is precluded. This phenomenon is illustrated by claims to the existence of

A thing whose identity will never be known.

An idea that has never occurred to anybody.

A person whom everyone had utterly forgotten.

An occurrence that no one has ever mentioned.

An integer that is never individually specified.

These items are *referentially inaccessible*: to indicate them concretely and specifically as bearers of the predicate at issue is straightaway to unravel them as so-characterized items.[1] Yet one cannot but acknowledge that there are such items, notwithstanding our inability to identify them.

The concept of an applicable but nevertheless noninstantiable predicate comes to view at this point. Such a predicate F will be such that its realization is not exemplifiable. For while it holds in the abstract that this property is indeed exemplified—so that $(\exists u)Fu$ will be true—nevertheless the very manner of its specification renders it impossible to specify any particular individual u_0 such that Fu_0 obtains. Such predicates are "vagrant" in the sense of *having no known address or fixed abode.* Despite their having applications, these cannot be specifically instanced—they cannot be pinned down and located in a particular spot. And on this basis we may define:

> F is a *vagrant* predicate if $(\exists u)Fu$ is true while nevertheless
> Fu_0 is false for each and every specifically identified u_0.

Predicates of this sort will be such that—while general principles show that there indeed are items to which they apply, nevertheless it lies in their very nature that such items should ever be concretely instantiated.[2] It lies in the very make-up of their specification that when F is vagrant, then Fx_0 is a contradiction in terms where x is a specifically identified item. Thus $x_0\,Fx_0$ is not merely a counterfactual supposition but an incoherent, meaningless contention.

Many specific examples of vagrant predicates have already been given. So it is clear that:

—being a vagrant predicate

is itself not a vagrant predicate. Indeed, one salient illustration of this phenomenon is that afforded by the thematic issue of the present book, the idea of

—being a fact that is altogether unknowable.

After all, to characterize something as an instance of factuality is through this very circumstance to claim to know it.

Suppose now that the world's processes are such that certain occurrences leave no trace whatsoever, and suppose further that such occurrences ongoingly happen from time to time—beginning well prior to the emergence of intelligence in the cosmos. Then there will be an ever-expanding body of fact unknowable to the world's inquirers. Such traceless occurrence provides for one pathway to unknowable fact. But of course this sort of thing hinges contingently on the world's modus operandi, unlike the predicative vagrancy of the preceding examples.

It is accordingly necessary to distinguish contingent from necessary vagrancy. With necessarily vagrant predicates, however, specific inapplicability obtains as a matter of principle. The following afford some further illustrations of this phenomenon:

—being an ever-unstated (proposition, theory, and so on).

—being a never-mentioned topic (idea, object, and so on).

—being a truth (a fact) no one has ever realized (learned, stated).

—being the perpetuation of a perfect crime (i.e., one whose commitment goes totally undetected).

—being an issue no one has thought about since the sixteenth century.

It is the *necessary* vagrancy of such examples that is of particular concern in our present deliberations because it affords a pathway to necessary unknowability.

2. GENERAL VS. SPECIFIC KNOWLEDGE AND THE IMPACT OF VAGRANCY
In the abstract and formalistic reasonings of logic or mathematics—where predicates are cast in the language of abstraction—cognitive operators of the sort at issue in predicative vagrancy simply have no place. Here one will never encounter vagrant predicates. For in such contexts we affirm *what* we know but never claim *that* we know. However, with matters of empirical fact the situation can be very different.

In those epistemic cases that concern us now, cognitive inaccessibility is built into the specification at issue. Here being instantiated stands in direct logical conflict with the characterization at issue, as with:

—being a sandgrain of which no one ever took note.

—being a person who has passed into total oblivion.

—being a never-formulated question.

—being an idea no one any longer mentions.

To identify such an item (in the manner now at issue) is thereby to unravel its specifying characterization.[3]

The difference between predicate vagrancy and its contrary mirrors the contrast between:

- *generic knowledge*: It is known *that something* has: $K(\exists x)Fx$
- *specific knowledge*: *something that* has F is known about, that is, one knows *of* something in specific that *it* has F: $(\exists x)KFx$

Here K can be read as "It is known that" (or alternatively as "I know that").

In the former case it is merely known that F has application; in the latter case one is in a position to identify a specific example of F-application—to adduce a *known instance* of F. From the logical standpoint, then, the issue comes down to the relative placement of the existential quantifier and the cognitive operator.

In this way, the difference between the two modes of knowledge is particularly marked in the case of existential quantification. For when we have:

$$(\exists x)\ KFx$$

then there will have to be some particular x for which we have KFx. But if all we have is:

$$K(\exists x)Fx$$

then this is not the case. For now there may just be no particular individual at all for which we know that F appertains specifically to it. For example, I doubtless know on the basis of general principles that everyone who was on the Appian Way on the fatal Ides of March was in Italy at the time. But I may well not know of anyone in specific of whom this was the case.

And it is in just this manner that vagrancy manifests itself. Item-specific knowledge is at issue when we know something in specific regarding a particular object. By contrast, if all we have is that all things of a certain type have central features—possibly without even realizing that a certain particular object is of this type (or indeed event this object exists)—then we do not have specific knowledge of it. For to obtain KFx_0 from $K(\forall x)(x \in S \rightarrow Fx)$ we would need $K(x_0 \in S)$—and a fortiori also $KE!x_0$.

The knowledge operator K is of the essence here.[4] What is pivotal in all of these cases of vagrant predicates is that they involve a specification which—like identification, comprehension, formulation, mention, and so on—is fundamentally epistemic—something that can only be performed by a creature capable of cognitive and communicative performances. This is readily established. Let F be a vagrant predicate. Since we then by hypothesis have it that $(\exists u)Fu$ is true, there is clearly nothing impossible about being F-possessing as such. Ontologically speaking there are, by hypothesis, items to which F applies; what is infeasible is only providing an instance—a specific example or illustration. The impossibility lies not in "being an F" as such but in "being a concrete/instantiated F." The problem is not with the indefinite "*something* is an F" but with the specific "*this* is an F." Difficulty lies not with F-hood as such, but with its specific application—not with the ontology of there being an F but with the epistemology of its apprehension in individual cases.

A particularly radical version of predicative vagrancy would arise if we were to have both $K(\forall x)Fx$ and $\sim(\exists x)KFx$. Thus I might know that all descendents of Attila the Hun carry his DNA without knowing of any single particular individual that does so.

Vagrant predicates betoken the unavoidability of areas of ignorance and unknowability. In this regard, they are emblematic of the fact that one of the most critical but yet problematic areas of inquiry relates to knowledge regarding our own cognitive shortcomings. To be sure there is no problem with the idea that Q is a question we cannot answer. But it is next to impossible to get a more definite fix on our own ignorance, because in order even to know that there is a certain particular fact that we do not know, we would have to know the item at issue to be a fact, and just this is, by hypothesis, something we do not know.[5]

And these considerations bear directly on our present deliberations. For we here maintain that there indeed are truths that nobody can possibly know, so that we have $K(\exists p)(p \ \& \sim\!\lozenge Kp)$. Yet we acknowledge that there is no possibility of *illustrating* this, seeing that the thesis

$$(\exists p)K(p \ \& \sim\!\lozenge Kp)$$

is untenable on grounds of self-inconsistency. We clearly cannot interchange that K with its associated $(\exists p)$.

One must accordingly acknowledge that there is a crucial difference between the indefinite "I know that there is some fact that I do not (or cannot) know" and the specific "Such and such is a fact of which I know that I do not know it." The first is unproblematic but the second not, seeing that to know of something that it is a fact I must know it as such so that what is at issue is effectively a contradiction in terms.

3. IDENTITY AND IDENTIFIABILITY
Consider the predicate:

—is an existing item that is not identifiable (i.e., is something whose identity cannot be specified).

It is clear that this predicate would not be conceptually viable—would be self-introductory and logically inconsistent—if the thesis that "To be is to be identifiable" held well. But this principle is deeply problematic. No doubt everything whatsoever has an identity. (As Bishop Buter insisted, "Everything is what it is and not another thing.") But to *have* an identity and to be identifiable—that is, to have an identity that can be specified—are quite different things.

Letting i(F,x) abbreviate "The identifying formula F identifies the individual x," let us compare and contrast:

(1) $K(\forall x)(\exists F)i(F,x)$ "We know that all individuals have an identifier (i.e., have an identity)."
(2) $(\forall x)K(\exists F)i(F,x)$ "For any and every individual, we know of it that it has an identifier (i.e., has an identity)."
(3) $(\forall x)(\exists F)Ki(F,x)$ "Every individual has a *known* identifier—i.e., is identifiable through a *specifiable* identifier."

Here (1) is unproblematic. But (2) and (3) are simply untenable. They both claim that there is something we know *in specific of all individuals*—a claim which, given the infinitude at issue, is simply false. Having an identity and being identifiable by a specifying formula—that is, having a specifiable identifier—are different things altogether. And while the former may be cast in the role of logico-conceptual truism, the latter is flatly false.

That having an identity and being identifiable—that is, having an identity that can actually be specified—are very different things should be evident from the consideration that item-specification has to proceed linguistically so that only a denumerable number of item-specifications can ever be developed. On this (linguistic) basis we are restricted to a denumerable number of item specifications. So if existence and identifiability were coordinate—if "To be is to be identifiable"—then we would be constrained to say that only a denumerable number of real number can exist. And this would be absurd.

At this stage someone might be tempted to offer the following objection: Will not superlatives provide one a means to particularizing those vagrant predicates? What about the move from

—is a person never thought of by anyone since the days of Napoleon

to

—is the oldest person never thought of by anyone since the days of Napoleon.

Will this not provide us with an escape from vagrancy's unlocalizabiilty?

Alas, this seemingly promising tactic will not work. Because outright identification requires uniqueness there is never any assurance that no ties will be encountered here. And if we change the location to "is one of the oldest persons . . ." we are back on the grips of vagrancy.

4. COUNTING

Such particles have no specifiable extension. To count things is to apply a sort of mental tag to them. Now in playing the game of tag you can't tag what you can't catch. And analogously, in counting you can't count what you can't identify.

Mathematical logicians coordinate predicates with the set of objects satisfying them. For then, the set of items having the property F—symbolically $\{x: F\}$—mirrors in *extension* what this predicate represents in *intension*. But this Principle of Extensionality clearly will not work with vagrant predicates whose instances we cannot identify.

And so one cannot possibly count the membership of the "extension" of such a predicate and assign a cardinal number to it. For counting requires identification—where items cannot be identified, they cannot be counted either. And so while a vagrant predicate may well be multiply applicable, the number of those instantiations cannot possibly be counted. Vagrancy thus puts a new sense of uncountability on the agenda—a sense we had perhaps better indicate as noncountability, seeing that "uncountably many" generally connotes immensity.

It is important to note that even when *counting* is impossible, it is nevertheless often possible to make quantitative comparisons. Thus consider the following vagrant predicate:

—being a now totally forgotten member of the [small, long extinct] Zonga tribe.

Obviously this is bound to have a smaller range of potential application than the predicate:

—is now a totally forgotten human being.

There are, clearly, fewer instantiations of the former predicate than of the latter—notwithstanding the impersonability of doing any counting here.

5. THE CENTRALITY OF EPISTEMIC INVOLVEMENT

Predicative vagrancy has interesting ramifications. To establish vagrancy for a predicate F one needs to show that while there indeed are F-instantiating items, nevertheless they cannot be specifically identified, so that their status as such is never known. But since some items do indeed bear vagrant predicates it follows that one's ignorance about facts is something about which one can have only generic and not specific knowledge. I can know about my ignorance only abstractly at the level of indefiniteness (*sub ratione generalitatis*), but I cannot know it in concrete detail. I can meaningfully hold that two and two's being four is a *claim* (or a *purported* fact) that I do not know to be the case, but cannot meaningfully maintain that two and two's being four is an *actual* fact that I do not know to be the case. To maintain a fact as fact is to assert knowledge of it: in maintaining p as a fact one claims to know that p. One can know *that* one does not know various truths, but is not in a position to *identify* any of the specific truths one does not know. In sum, I can have general but not specific knowledge about my ignorance, although my knowledge about *your* ignorance would be unproblematic in this regard.[6]

We have embarked on a quest for facts that are in principle unknowable as a matter of inexorable necessity. And it is, or should be, clear that the only facts of this sort are those that achieve this status as a matter of *conceptual necessity*. That is, such facts themselves must be identified or specified in such a way that renders their cognitive inaccessibility is an unavoidable *fait accompli*: their unknowability must be a *conceptual* feature built into the very make-up of the conceptual specification of the item(s) at issue.

And so, something noteworthy is bound to be going on here, namely that the noninstantiability at issue with predicative vagrancy is built overtly into the very specification of the predicate involved. Being uninstantiable stands in direct logical conflict with the characterization at issue, exactly as with:

—being a person who has passed into total oblivion.

—being a never-formulated question.

—being an idea no one any longer mentions.

Actually identifying such an item would thereby automatically unravel its specifying characterization.[7] (And, of course, the unknowability at issue here is of a genus that includes various sorts of obviously interrelated species: unidentifiability, unspecifiability, unexemplifiability, uninstantiability, and the like.)

And just here is where vagrant predicates come into it. There may well be—nay doubtless are—individuals that bear vagrant predicates. But one cannot possibly provide an example. The question "What is an example of an item that bears a vagrant predicate?" affords a vivid illustration of an inherently unanswerable question. It asks for the impossible. For if some specifiable item *A* did have that predicate *F* which, *ex hypothesi*, is to be vagrant, then *ex hypothesi* that predicate would not be vagrant. And this invokes a contradiction. There is something about a vagrant predicate *F* that renders it incompatible with knowledge, and which, in consequence, endows it with inherently epistemic involvements. What is pivotal for predicative vagrancy is that such predicates involve a specification that denies something which—like identification, comprehension, formulation, mention, etc.—is fundamentally epistemic: something that can only be performed by a creature capable of cognitive and communicative performances. The uninstantiability of F's being a vagrant predicate lies not in regard to "there being an F" as such but in "being a concretely/instantiated F." The problem lies not with F-possession as such, but with its specific application—not with the ontology of there being an F but with the epistemology of its apprehension in individual cases. The long and short of it is that vagrant predicates involve a specification which—like identification, comprehension, formulation, mention, and the like—is fundamentally epistemic—something that is a cognitive performance that can only be managed by an intelligent creature.

* * *

While unknowable facts can never be specifically instantiated, they can, nevertheless, be categorized. Contingent unknowability roots in the unforseeability of the future, in the limited nature of the reasoning resources available to knowers, and also in the limits of theorizing imposed by the structure of their experience. Necessity-based unknowability roots in predicative vagrancy.

Overall, we have surveyed four pathways to unknowability:

Developmental unpredictability

Varificational surdity

Ontological excess

Predicative vagrancy

With developmental unpredictability there is an unrealizable demand for present access to futurity. With surdity we require an infinite number of distinct cognitive acts. And with ontological excess a demand for knowledge would overreach the limits of the possible. With vagrancy we demand realization of an inherent impossibility. In each case there is unavoidable unknowability—and for good reason.

NOTES

1. We can, of course, refer to such individuals and even to some extent describe them. But what we cannot do is *identify* them.

2. A uniquely characterizing description on the order of "the tallest person in the room" will single out a particular individual without specifically identifying him.

3. To be sure, one could (truthfully) say something like "The individual who prepared Caesar's breakfast on the fatal Ides of March is now totally unknown." But the person at issue here goes altogether unknown, that is, he or she is alluded to but not specified—individuated but not concretely identified. So I cannot appropriately claim to know *who* the individual at issue is but only at best *that* a certain individual is at issue.

4. Note that it could just as well be read "I know that" or "*X* knows that."

5. The thesis "I know that *p* is a known fact that I don't know" comes to:

$$Ki[(\exists x)Kxp \ \& \sim Kip] \quad \text{(here } i = \text{oneself)}$$

This thesis entails my knowing both $(\exists x)Kxp$ and $\sim Kip$. But the former circumstance entails Kip, and this engenders a contradiction. Of course "knowing a certain particular fact" involves not just knowing THAT *there is* a fact, but also calls for knowing WHAT *that fact is.*

6. Accordingly, there is no problem about "$t_\emptyset$ is a truth *you* don't know," although I could not then go on to claim modestly that "You know everything that I do." For the contentions $\sim Kyt_\emptyset$ and $(\forall t)(Kit \supset Kyt)$ combine to yield $\sim Kit_\emptyset$, which conflicts with the claim $Kit_\emptyset$ that I stake in claiming *t*o as a truth.

7. To be sure, one could (truthfully) say something like "The individual who prepared Caesar's breakfast on the fatal Ides of March is now totally unknown." But the person at issue here is merely alluded to but not specified—individuated but not concretely identified. So I cannot appropriately claim to know *who* the individual at issue is but only at best *that* a certain individual is at issue.

7

An Application to Paradoxology: Vagueness

1. THE SORITES PARADOX AND ITS PROBLEMS

Vagueness is a prime source of paradox. For vague terms have a more or less well-defined central core of application surrounded by a large penumbra of indefiniteness and uncertainty. And because when a term T is vague its negation non-T will automatically also be so, there will inevitably be a nebulous region of ambivalent overlap between T situations and non-T situations where matters seem to stand both ways so that a paradoxical inconsistency arises.

The most familiar ways of addressing the well-known paradoxes of vagueness call for the employment of heavy machinery, requiring either a nonstandard mode of reasoning (adopting a fuzzy logic, abandoning the Law of Excluded Middle) or a nonstandard semantics (abandoning Principles of Bivalence, accepting truth-value gaps), or both. By contrast, the presently contemplated approach to vagueness proposes to leave the machinery of classical logic and standard semantics pretty much intact, and to let the burden of paradox resolution be carried by strictly epistemological considerations. Unavailable information rather than deficient theorizing is here asked to bear the brunt.

The problem of vagueness has a long history. Among the ancient Greeks, Eubulides of Megara (b. ca. 400 BC) was the most prominent and influential member of the Megarian school of dialecticians as whose head he succeeded its founder, Euclid of Megara, a pupil of Socrates.[1] Eubulides did more to promote concern for the pardoxicality of vagueness than any other single thinker in the history of the subject. He is credited with seven important paradoxes: *The Liar* (*pseudomenos*), *The Overlooked Man* (*dialanthanôn*), *Electra and her Brother*, *The Masked Man* (*egkekalummenos*), *The Heap* (*sôritês*), *The Horns* (*keratinês*), and *The Bald Man* (*phalakros*). All of them pivot on issues of vagueness or equivocation.

What here particularly concerns us among these puzzles is the "Paradox of the Heap"—the *Sorites Paradox* (from the Greek *sôros* = heap)—which is posed in the following account:

> A single grain of sand is certainly not a heap. Nor is the addition of a single grain of sand enough to transform a non-heap into a heap: when we have a collection of grains of sand that is not a heap, then adding but one single grain will not create a heap. And so by adding successive grains, moving from 1 to 2 to 3 and so on, we will *never* arrive at a heap. And yet we know full well that a collection of 1,000,000 grains of sand is a heap, even if not an enormous one.[2]

Throughout the ages, theorists have diagnosed the problem at issue here by locating its difficulty in vagueness, thus assimilating it to a vast panoply of similar puzzles (example: a new-sharpened bread knife is not dull, and cutting a single additional slice of bread with a knife that is not dull will not dull it. Yet when the knife has cut a million slices, it will be dull. Or again: if you are still on time for an appointment, the delay of a nanosecond will not make you late, and yet a great multitude of such delays engenders lateness). The guiding idea is that in all such cases the pivotal concept—be it "heap" or "bald" or "dull" or "late"—is vague in that there is no sharp and definite cut-off point between the IN and OUT of its application. The "borderline" at issue is not exactly that, but rather a blurred band that is imprecise, nebulous, indefinite, inexact, or some such. And just this is the course of difficulty.

To come to grips with the core to the problem, let $H(n)$ abbreviate "a unified collection of n grains of sands is a heap." We can then formalize the premisses of the Sorites paradox as follows:

(1) $\sim H(2)$ ("Two grains do not form a heap.")
(2) $(\forall n)[\sim H(n) \rightarrow \sim H(n + 1)]$ ("If n grains are insufficient to form a heap, adding just one will not mend matters.")
(3) $H(1,000,000)$ ("A million grains will form a heap.")

Starting out from premiss (1), repeated application of (2) will yield the negation of (3). So our three premisses are inconsistent. And yet individually considered they all look to be plausible. Hence the paradox. How is it to be resolved?

Since premises (1) and (3) are uncontestable, it is clearly premiss (2) that will have to bear the burden of doubt. But in rejecting (2) we will, by classical logic's Law of the Excluded Middle, be saddled with its negation, namely:

(4) $(\exists n)\ [\sim H(n)\ \&\ H(n + 1)]$

But now if *this* is accepted, grave problems seem to follow, for by in the widely favored Substitutional Construal of Existential Quantification we will have the principle:

(S) If $(\exists x)Fx$, then there must be a particular value x_0
of the variable x for which Fx_0 obtains.

And if this is so, then there will be an identifiable transition point—a particular and specific integer N for which not-(2) obtains. And so we have:

(5) For some particular, specific integer N there obtains: $\sim H(N)\ \&\ H(N + 1)$

This upshot appears to be altogether counterintuitive and unacceptable. But nevertheless we seem to have a natural and inevitable transit by standard logic from the rejection of (2) to an acceptance of (4) and thence via (S) to (5). Where does this unpalatable result leave us?

To block this chain of reasoning most theorists have proposed to embargo the move from not-(2) to (4) by some maneuver or other. Mathematical intuitionists propose to accomplish this by prohibiting the move from the refutation of a universal claim to the maintenance of an existential one. Supporters of a "fuzzy" logic propose to abandon the classical laws of excluded middle and *tertium non datur*.

Against such approaches, however, the present discussion maintains the availability of another, logically far less radical alternative—an alternative to which we must in any case resort on other grounds. This alternative approach pivots on bringing the idea of vagrant predication into operation.

2. VAGUENESS AS VAGRANCY

Recall that a vagrant predicate F is one whose realization is noninstantiable because, while indeed exemplified, nevertheless the very manner of its specification renders it impracticable to *identify* any particular individual u_0 such that Fx_0 obtains. Accordingly:

> F is a *vagrant* predicate if $(\exists x)Fx$ is true, while nevertheless Fx_0 is bound to be false for each and every *specifically identified x_0*.

As already noted, such predicates as

—being a person who has passed into total oblivion

—being a never-formulated question

—being an idea no one any longer mentions

illustrate this phenomenon. Throughout such cases, specifically identified instantiation stands in direct logical conflict with the characterization at issue. To identify an item instantiating such a predicate is thereby to contradict its very characterization.[3]

With vagrant predicates the existence of exemplifications is an *ontological* fact, but it is offset by the no less firm *epistemological* fact that no such exemplifying instance can possibly ever be identified. They mark a cognitive divide between reality and our knowledge of it.

And now back to vagueness. Wherever it functions, there is no viable way of separating the INs from the OUTs. But here one can take either an ontological or an epistemic approach. The former effectively says "there is no definite boundary"; the latter says "there indeed is a definite boundary but there is no practicable way of locating it, no feasible way of noting where it lies." The one denies the existence, the other the identifiability of boundaries.

In the case of the heap paradox these opposites afford two possibilities. The one consists in flat-out denying the thesis:

$$(\exists n)[\sim H(n) \ \& \ H(n + 1)]$$

But yet another alternative approach proceeds by retaining this contention but blocking the move from it to:

(5) There is a particular, determinable value N of the viable n for which the preceding contention holds.

In effect we now bring the concept of vagrant predicates to bear. And by treating vagueness as vagrancy we effectively block the heap paradox and its congeners. For once that pivotal predicate which characterizes a transition from nonheap to heap is seen as vagrant, the whole idea of isolating that problematic transition value vanishes from the scene. The two conceptions—vagueness and vagrancy—can thus be seen as functionally symbiotic.

To be sure, an approach to vagueness along these lines involves a nonstandard handling of the issue of a transition point between the INs and the OUTs. For the traditional approach to such boundaries is that of the ontological contention that they do not exist as such (i.e., as actual boundaries), but are to be replaced by penumbral regions (whose boundaries themselves are penumbral in turn—all the way through). And this means that there will fail to be a "fact of the matter" in regard to being IN or being OUT. Here the logical principle of *tertium non datur* has to be abandoned.

By contrast, our present vagrancy-based approach takes an *epistemological* line. It does not call for denying that there is such a thing as a (classically conceived) boundary. And it does not deny that *any* given item either is IN or not. In sum it does not conflict with the idea that *facts* are at issue here. But what it does insist upon is that these facts are *in principle undeterminable*. The predicate

—being the boundary between IN and OUT

is classed vagrant.

3. SOME FURTHER DETAIL ON VAGUENESS

With vagueness there will be a region of indeterminacy as between the INs and the OUTs, but that this region is, as it were, penumbral. It will not have sharp, razor-edged boundaries but must be nebulous, with the boundary between IN and INDETERMINATE (and again between INDETERMINATE and OUT) being comparably indeterminate (penumbral, "fuzzy") once more. The absence of clear transitional borders will hold "all the way through," so to speak. For this reason, a three-valued logic of TRUE, FALSE, and INDETERMINATE will not do the job that is needed here. Any "fuzzy logic" adequate to the taste of accommodating vagueness must be infinite-valued, with never-ending room for shades and gradations. Pretty complex logical machinery needs to be brought to bear.

However, the now-envisioned approach to vagueness pivots on the critical distinction between the located and the locatable. As it views the matters, there indeed is (ontologically, so to speak) a sharp and clear boundary between the INs and the OUTs, but there is (epistemically, so to speak) no possible way of locating it. In taking this line, the recourse to predicative vagueness shifts the burden from the ontological to the epistemological side of things. The advantage of such a strategy is that it makes it possible to keep in place a classically binary logic and foregoes abandoning the classical principles of excluded middle and *tertium non datur*. The only innovation needed—and one that is required in any case—is to accept the prospect of vagrant predication.

What we have here is the anomaly of a *point of demarcation* (as between being a heap and a nonheap, a sharp or dull knife, a same-color patch and a different-color patch)—an IN and an OUT, is inherently unidentifiable. Such a point exists—so it is held—but remains inherently unidentifiable. Viewed from this perspective, vagueness emerges as an artifact of insufficient cognition. The indefiniteness at issue is now ascribed not to reality's indecisiveness, but rather to certain of our concepts— specifically those at issue with vagrant predicates.

And so, while the standard view of vagueness sees the separation of vaguely bounded regions as a matter of unlimitedness—the result of absent boundaries—the present nonstandard approach combines an insistence on the *existence* of boundaries with an insistence on their (epistemic) unlocatability. The positions are very different but their net effect is in one respect the same: no locatable boundaries.

There is a multitude of examples of objects that are real but unidentifiable. As regards the past, there is many a saying in circulation whose inaugurator nobody can by now identify. As regards the future, the person who will win the 2020 U.S. presidential election is for-sure currently alive and active among us, but cannot yet possibly be identified. And as regards abstractors there must exist an unprovable arithmetical theorem whose Gödel number is the lowest—but this too cannot be identified. Our present treatment of vagueness extends this actual—but unidentifiable—approach to those otherwise nebulous boundaries involved with vagueness.

After all, one must avoid equating nonspecificability with nonexistence. For as we have seen time and again, vagrant predicates, though uninstantiable by us, need not in themselves be uninstantiated. There will certainly be (some) totally forgotten people, though none of us can possibly provide an example. And analogously it could be held that there indeed is a sharp boundary between heaps and nonheaps (of sandgrains of a given size) even though it is in principle impossible ever to say just where this boundary lies. It is concealed in a cognitive blind spot, as it were.[4] For while, from such a perspective, there indeed is a transition, and even a transition point, nevertheless this is not something that can possibly be fixed upon; it cannot possibly be identified.

Consider, for example, a color strip of distinct compartments as per:

c_1	c_2	c_3	c_4				

where adjacent compartments are visually color-indistinguishable

$$(\forall i)[P(c_i) = P(c_i + 1)]$$

Nevertheless, the situation is such that there will be notable differences among sufficiently remote compartments. Thus we will have:

$$P(c_1) \uparrow P(c_{100})$$

But where is one to place the transition between $P(c_i)$ and $P(c_{100})$? Where does $P(c_i)$ end and where does $P(c_{100})$ begin? We have exactly the same problem as with heaps. And exactly the same sort of solution looms before us with a resort to predicative vagrancy able to do the needed work.[5]

Now on the present epistemic perspective, the crux of vagueness is that one knows that there is a transition point between IN and OUT, but cannot possibly manage to locate it. And just this represents a fundamental aspect of vagueness in general: there just is no way of saying at just what point predicate-applicative begins and where it ends. We know that a crossover is eventually reached, but cannot possibly say just where it lies.

4. THE EPISTEMOLOGICAL TURN

Such treatment of vagueness takes the line that there indeed is a boundary between the INs and the OUTs in matters of vagueness, so that one can maintain:

(I) $(\exists B)$ [B marks the boundary between IN and OUT]

Nevertheless, there is no way of *fixing* this boundary, no way of determining just exactly where it lies. There is no prospect of identifying a particular value of B_0 of the variable B such that

(II) B_0 marks the boundary between IN and OUT.

From the ontological/existential point of view the existence of a boundary is acknowledged as per (I). But from an epistemological/cognitive point of view any and all possibility of locating this boundary—of determining or specifying it—is precluded.

Exactly this is the characteristic situation of predicative vagrancy. As adumbrated above, the crucial difference here is that between the acceptable:

$K(\exists B)(B$ mark the boundary between IN and OUT)

and the unacceptable:

$(\exists B) K(B$ mark the boundary between IN and OUT)

And in viewing the matter as one of vagueness, the existence of a boundary point is conceded, but its specifiability is denied.

So viewed, the ultimate responsibility for the indefiniteness of vagueness thus lies not with what is at issue in our discourse but in the imperfection of our knowledge: "the fault is not in our stars, but in ourselves" in that our very vocabulary precludes exact knowledge.

The crux of the presently contemplated approach to vagueness is that the descriptive qualifier "is a transition point between IN and OUT" is to be seen as a vagrant predicate—it applies someplace, but we know not where. And the qualifier "is to the left of the transition point" is sometimes *undecidable*: sometimes it clearly applies, sometimes it clearly does not, and sometimes it falls into the indeterminate "just can't say" region. (The boundaries of that region will themselves be specified by vagrant predicates.) In principle undecidable propositions occur not just in mathematics but in the factual domain as well.

But just what is the pay-off difference between saying that there just is no boundary and saying that there is one but it is altogether unidentifiable? Simply and exactly the difference between the epistemic and the existential. It is one thing to say that there is nothing in the box and quite another to say that there is no way for anyone to know what it contains. (Think of the magic box—impenetrable to external scanning—whose content is annihilated by opening the lid.)

But how can one personally make sense of the idea of an exact boundary for vague terminology? Perhaps one way of doing so is to resort to a myth—the myth of an Ultimate Decider, a sort of language-fixing Academie Mondiale charged with creating a language from which vague and equivocal terms have been expunged. Now here the working groups charged with providing a functional revision of the term "heap" carries out its deliberations and comes up with an exact cutoff. There would eventually emerge the idea that (1) there is indeed to be a fixed, vagueness-removing boundary, while nevertheless (2) there just is no practicable way for us ever to find it out. On this basis, the unknowability associated with vagueness is subsumed under that relating to the future.

Such a view of the matter may seem to be a bit far-fetched, but at least it provides a scenario that renders the idea conveniently intelligible.

5. RAMIFICATIONS

Our claims regarding reality generally fall short in point of accuracy and detail for reasons ultimately rooted in our human condition as beings whose knowledge is mediated by language. A descriptive term is *equivocal* if its application invites the question: "In what sense?" (example: *gay* or *crooked*). A descriptive term is *vague* if its application invites the question: "Of what sort or kind?" (example: *vehicle* or *metal*). A descriptive term is *ambiguous* if its application invites the question: "In what mode, respect, or manner?" (example: *instructive* or *incompetent*). A term is *inexact* or *imprecise* if its application invites the question: "In what degree or to what extent?" (example: *large* or *old*). Moreover, a descriptive term is *figurative* when it is in some respect metaphorical or analogical, so as to make the question: "Just how is this so?" As such cases indicate, human communication is replete with unclarity and inexactness, ever admitting further questions about the purport of what has been said. While reality itself is interrogatively complete, our thought and discourse about it certainly is not: We are constantly constrained to use loose terminology and fill our discourse with expressions on the order of "roughly," "approximately," "something like," "in the neighborhood of," "in his seventies," "some six feet tall," and so on. This prominence in our discussions of indecisiveness—of vagueness, equivocation, and the rest—has larger ramifications.

Consider, for example, an inscription that reads:

$$R\nu T$$

We just cannot make that middle letter out. On the basis of general principles we can maintain:

(1) ν must be a vowel.
(2) Only A, O, U are real possibilities.

Of course if we had a context we could go further:

—He was bitten by a RνT.

—He left it in the street to RνT.

—He got stuck in a RνT.

Context often will, or at least can, pave a way to determination here. But in the absence of a context all we can say is

(1) We know that the missing letter is one of A, O, U:

$$K(\nu = A \bigvee \nu = O \bigvee \nu = U)$$

(2) But we do not know which of them in particular it is:

$$\sim K(\nu = A) \ \& \ \sim K(\nu = O) \ \& \ \sim K(\nu = U)$$

In sum, what we have here is the typical vagrancy situation of

$$K(\exists x)(v = x) \ \& \ \sim(\exists x)K(v = x)$$

We know *that* v is one of A, O, U, but have no clue as to which of this trio that problematic v actually is. It is clear on this basis the predicate:

—being the letter represented by v

is (contingently) vagrant.

And so with equivocation too we have a situation that can be analyzed in terms of predicative vagrancy. And the situation of vagueness can be seen as simply a more ordered version of this same phenomena. In effect, both vagueness and equivocation can be seen as yet another mode of unknowability.

6. WHY VAGUENESS PAYS

The fact of it is that reality is so vastly complex in its mode of operation that a shortfall of detail in our description of it is an inevitable reality. In characterizing the real, the indecisiveness of vagueness is not a failing but an inevitability. And so, one reason for our tolerance of congeners lies in our having little choice about it.

But that is not the end of it. For the fact of it is that vagueness also plays a critically important role in human communication. For it is certainly important that a descriptive characterization be true and vagueness factually does not stop such a statement from being true. If we could not describe the grass of our experience as vaguely green or indeed even merely greenish, but only had the choice of a myriad exact shades of green, color communication would virtually grind to a halt. If we had to decide when "rock" leaves off and "boulder" begins, we would be in difficulty. Despite its manifest problems, vagueness is immensely useful.

And so in the final analysis we tolerate vagueness because we have no choice, and we do so gladly not just because it is convenient, but also because greater detail is generally not needed in the relevant contexts of operation. (We do not need to know whether the approaching storm will bring 1 or 1.5 inches of rain for deciding whether or not to take an umbrella.)[6]

NOTES

1. Pretty well all that is known about Eubulides derives from Diogenes Laertius, *Lives of the Philosophers*, Bk. II, sects. 106–20. See Zeller, *Philosophie der Griechen*, vol. II/1, 246.

2. On this paradox and its ramifications see Chapter 2 of R. M. Sainsbury, *Paradoxes*, 2nd ed. (Cambridge: Cambridge University Press, 1995), 23–51. Originally the paradox also had a somewhat different form, as follows: Clearly 1 is a small number. And if n is a small number so is $n + 1$. But this leads straightway to having to say that an obviously large number (say a zillion billion) is a small number. (See Prantl, *Geschichte der Logik im Abendlande*, vol. I, 54.) Note that the paradox could equally well be developed regressively (i.e., from heapness by substantive regression) as progressively from nonheapness by additive progression. The former regressive style of reasoning is called Galenic after Galen (AD 129–c. 210) who wrote prolifically on logic; the latter progressive style is called Goclenic after Randolph Goclenius (1547–1628) who discussed the matter in his *Introduction to Aristotle's Organon. Isagoge in Organon Aristotelis* (Frankfurt, 1598).

3. To be sure one could (truthfully) say something like "The individual who prepared Caesar's breakfast on the fatal Ides of March is now totally unknown." But the person at issue here goes altogether unknown, that is, he or she is alluded to but not specified—individuated but not concretely identified. So I cannot appropriately claim to know *who* the individual at issue is but only at best *that* a certain individual is at issue.

4. For further, different cases of this general sort see Roy E. Sorensen, *Blindspots* (Oxford: Clarendon Press, 1988).

5. This shows that transitional continuity is not the core of the problem: the selfsame situation can confront us in the discrete case.

6. Further information on paradoxes can be found in the author's *Paradoxes* (Chicago: Open Court, 2001). An extensive literature is cited there, including: J. C. Beall, ed., *Liars and Heaps: New Essays on Paradox* (Oxford: Clarendon Press, 2003); L. Burns, *Vagueness: An Investigation into Natural Languages and the Sorites Paradox* (Dordrecht: Reidel, 1991); V. McGee, *Truth, Vagueness, and Paradox* (Indianapolis: Hackett, 1990); R. M. Sainsbury, *Paradoxes*, 2nd ed. (Cambridge: Cambridge University Press, 1995) [see especially chapter 2, "Vagueness: The Paradox of the Heap"].

8

Metaphysical Ramifications

1. HOW DOES THE PRESENCE OF INTELLIGENCE CHANGE THE WORLD?

The phenomenon of absolutely unknowable facts has interesting metaphysical ramifications. For since there indeed are such facts, there should be an explanation of the reason why—of how it comes to be that the world is such that some facts about it are simply unavailable to its intelligences. But what could this explanation be?

Certainty is hard to achieve in philosophical matters. But one thing is for sure. The universe contains intelligent beings. Not, perhaps, *very* intelligent beings, but nevertheless beings who not only have the capacity for intelligent agency but do actually make use of it some of the time.

How did such beings get to be there? Essentially by evolutionary processes. First there was cosmic evolution through the developing complexity and diversification of physical process, and then biological evolution by variation and natural selection. And intelligent beings ultimately emerged—presumably because there was a viable niche for beings whose survival advantage came through intelligence rather than a variety of alternatives. Thereafter, those intelligent beings were able themselves to bring cultural and social evolution into play.

Evolution is nature's innovator. Cosmic, biological, and cultural evolution all bring massive novelties in their wake. There were no laws of chemistry in the first nanosecond of the universe after the big bang—only a boiling soup of subatomic stuff in which chemicals had not yet emerged. And similarly there were no laws of cellular biology in the first billion years of our universe's existence, nor laws of macroeconomics in its first ten billion. With the emergence of new processes, new forms of being ongoingly come into existence, and new modes of process—and thereby lawfulness—arise in their wake.

The problem of just how intelligence changes the universe is a philosophical issue which (rather surprisingly) few philosophers have addressed. It is an issue that can be posed in many ways: What sort of massively significant novelty has come into existence with the evolutionary emergence of intelligence? What fundamental difference is there between an intelligence-containing universe and its intelligence-lacking congeners? What difference does intelligence make to the nature of things? All of these questions highlight varying aspects of one selfsame interesting and intriguing issue.

Was the emergence of intelligence fortuitous or unavoidable? Many theorists believe that it was inevitable because intelligence is so effective a survival mechanism in a complex and changeable environment. But be this as it may, once intelligence gains a foothold in the universe—by whatever mechanism or means—what difference does its presence there make? What factors that would otherwise be missing come into existence in the world through the emergence of intelligence? This question sets the focal theme of the present chapter. It is predicated on the idea that nothing so fundamentally changes the world as the emergence of intelligent beings.

2. KEY INNOVATIONS

It is clear that many things can come into being only in the wake of intelligence. Some of them are trivial: only intelligent, mind-endowed beings can play tic-tac-toe. But here we are not concerned with such minutiae. Only large-scale macro-capacities are presently of interest. Our question is: What really massive and momentous capabilities that were previously absent does the evolutionary emergence of intelligence on the cosmic scene bring into being?

Clearly, here one answer is: *knowledge*—the capacity to formulate and process information. After all, knowing, like supposing, is something that only intelligent beings can possibly do. But on the other side of the coin there is also its contrary: ignorance! And indeed even *the inevitable ignorance of unknowable fact.*

With all of those necessarily inapplicable vagrant predicates that figured in the preceding chapter, it transpires that their case-specific noninstantiability—this salient inaccessibility to knowledge—is inherent in the very specification of what is at issue. Cognitive access here stands in direct logical conflict with the item characterizations that are at issue. For consider:

—being a person who has passed into total oblivion.

—being a never-formulated question.

—being an idea no one any longer mentions.

The knowledge-claim at issue in identifying such items will automatically un-ravel their specifying characterization.[1]

The existence of vagrant predicates brings it to light that once there are in-telligent beings to be dealt with, we will have before us questions which are genuine *insolubilia* in the medieval sense—question which indeed have a cor-rect answer, but one which cannot possibly be provided.

Many things come into the world only with the emergence of intelligent beings—knowing, supposing, planning, and sinning among them. And the in-evitable ignorance of predicative vagrancy must be added to the list.

3. THE FRUSTRATIONS OF INTELLIGENCE

As already noted, no one can answer the question:

What is an example of a question that will never be asked?

The epistemic vagrancy of such challenges defeats the effort of this world's fi-nite intelligences. But when it is said that a fact about the world is unknown or unknowable, there immediately arise two questions: "Which world?" and "By whom?"

The answer in both cases is straightforward: The world at issue is of course this world of ours—the one only available to us for factual knowledge rather than conjecture or supposition. And the question "By whom?" is of course to be answered: "By us—the intelligent beings who inhabit this world." World-external super- or supra-natural beings are not in question here. So when we speak of "facts being known" or of "questions being asked" we mean those be-ing construed with reference to this world's intelligent beings.

However, the issue of cognition is itself always in play with vagrancy: the unknowability of the facts at issue is built into their very specification. But since knowing and unknowing are something that only intelligent beings can do, it follows that such facts can meaningfully function in the world only after intelligence gains a foothold there. Granted, as long as only impersonal descriptive facts about the world are concerned, intelligence appears to have no inherently insuperable limits.

But what is pivotal in all of these cases of vagrant predicates is that they conceptually involve a specification which—like identification, comprehension, formulation, mention, etc.—is fundamentally epistemic since this sort of thing can only be possibly performed by a creature capable of cognitive and communicative performances. And viewed from this perspective, it is clear that predicative vagrancy springs into being only with the emergence of intelligence.

Barring the emergence of intelligence, the pivotal presuppositions of this issue are not met and these questions about the status of things in relation to the world's cognition-capable intelligences do not make sense. (There is no point in asking what nonexistent beings cannot do!)

Accordingly, a universe without intelligent beings will not be one that involucrates inherently unknowable facts. There is no reason of principle why intelligences should not be able to answer any and all strictly factual, reality-oriented questions about Nature's make-up and modus operandi. But what intelligence cannot manage to do is to get a comprehensive grip on itself—and in specific on its own limits as per the application of those vagrant predicates.

It is accordingly a noteworthy circumstance that only after the world comes to contain intelligent beings (finite intelligences) will there be facts about it that are not just *unknown* by those intelligences in the world but actually are even *unknowable* by them. As far as the impersonal facts about a mind are concerned, intelligence appears to enjoy a potential of "no holds barred." It is only the reaction of intelligence to fact that brings absolute unknowability into play.

And so—back to the beginning! How does the emergence of intelligence change the world? The short answer is—revolutionarily. For there is now a place for self-awareness in the scheme of things—self-awareness in matters of thought and in action through recognizing the limitations that will inevitably afflict the cognitive condition of finite beings. What intelligence cannot do is to get a comprehensive grip on itself—and in specific on its own limits. The irony of it is that the questions that defy the utmost efforts of intelligence are exactly those that relate to facts concerning the limits of its own operation—that the existence of intelligence in the world is a precondition of its own defeat.

Finite minds will always be imperfectly informed about their own limits and limitations. And since thinking and thought-guided acting are integral to the functional make-up of the world, there will be aspects of reality regarding which the world's intelligence must ever remain imperfectly informed. For, given the integration of thought into nature, an incompleteness of knowledge regarding the former unavoidably carries in its wake an incompleteness of knowledge also regarding the latter. Ironically, it is with the emergence of intelligence that the universe itself becomes imperfectly intelligible.

NOTE

1. To be sure, one could plausibly say something like "The individual who prepared Caesar's breakfast on the fatal Ides of March is now totally unknown." But is this true? After all, we have just taken note of this very individual. This seeming anomaly needs to be removed by a distinction. The individual has been alluded to but not specified—individuated but not concretely identified. So I cannot appropriately claim to know *who* the individual at issue is but only at best *that* a certain individual is at issue.

Appendix

On the Formal Logic of Unknowability

1. COMPLICATIONS OF UNKNOWABILITY

When one speaks of the necessary unknowability of certain facts, two different things can be at issue, namely that it is necessary that some facts remain unknown, or that there are some facts that are necessarily unknown. These reflect substantially different ideas, as a recourse to formalism makes clear. For the former comes to:

(1) $(\exists f)\sim Kf$ or equivalently $\sim\Diamond(\forall f)Kf$

while the second (far stronger) contention runs:

(2) $(\exists f)\sim Kf$ or equivalently $\sim(\forall f)\Diamond Kf$

The first obtains both because there are more truths than facts, and also because of the general principles of epistemic logic—as will soon be explained. The second of these also obtains, and does so on the basis of conceptual considerations regarding predicative vagrancy. That the second thesis is stronger than the first follows from the musical chairs analogy. For in this game it is indeed necessary that there be some player who is not seated, so that the analogue of (1) obtains. But there is no player who is necessarily not seated, so that the analogue of (2) does not obtain.

On grounds of mere self-inconsistency it is infeasible that someone should *know* some truth to represent an unknown fact:

$$(\exists x)(\exists p)\,Kx(p\ \&\ {\sim}(\exists y)Kyp) \text{ or equivalently } (\exists x)(\exists p)(Kxp\ \&\ Kx{\sim}(\exists y)Kyp)$$

This thesis must certainly be rejected on grounds of self-morality. But its weaker cousin to the effect that there indeed is such a thing as an unknown fact, that is

$$(\exists x)(\exists p)(p\ \&\ Kx{\sim}(\exists y)Kyp) \text{ or equivalently } (\exists x)(\exists p)(p\ \&\ Kx{\sim}(\forall y)Kyp)$$

is something very different—and perfectly practicable. One can know *that* there is an unknown truth; it is just that one cannot know *what* this is.

2. THE KNOWABILITY THESIS

Of late there has been increasing interest in the prospect of establishing the reality of unknown and indeed unknowable truth on the basis of very abstract and general considerations of epistemic logic, with several theorists contending that it can readily be demonstrated in this way that unknowable truth is an inescapable feature of our cognitive condition.[1]

The root source of this conviction lies in the circumstance that in 1963, the Yale logician Frederic B. Fitch published a brief paper (Fitch 1963) demonstrating on very general principles that there must be unknown truths. Since Fitch's paper did not stress the point and seemed preoccupied with other issues, this startling result lay dormant until attention was drawn to it in 1979 by W. D. Hart. Then in the 1980s deliberations regarding various ramifications of Fitch's insights were projected by J. J. MacIntosh, Richard Routley, Timothy Williamson, the present writer, and others. Let us consider where the issue of demonstrating the existence of unknowable truth is left in the light of this discussion and inquire into the status of the Knowability Thesis to the effect that: *any true proposition can possibly be known.* But just how is this to be substantiated?

Observe, to begin with, that this thesis is equivocal, and can bear different constructions according as one attaches an explanatory rider such as: "by any individual" or "by some individual or other." In fact, four alternatives arise:

   I. $(\forall t)(\forall x)\Diamond Kxt$ or equivalently $\sim(\exists t)(\exists x)\Box\sim Kxt$
  II. $(\forall t)\Diamond(\forall x)Kxt$ or equivalently $\sim(\exists t)\Box(\exists x)\sim Kxt$
 III. $(\forall t)(\exists x)\Diamond Kxt$ or equivalently $\sim(\exists t)(\forall x)\Box\sim Kxt$
 IV. $(\forall t)\Diamond(\exists x)Kxt$ or equivalently $\sim(\exists t)\Box(\forall x)\sim Kxt$

The four theses of this spectrum are not, of course, logically independent. It lies in the quantified modal logic of things that the following deductive relationships must obtain:

$$I \;\rightarrow\; III \;\rightarrow\; IV$$
$$II \;\nearrow$$

So the question now emerges: In which of these versions (if any) is the Knowability Thesis acceptable?[2] Our tactic here is to establish the untenability of IV, so that the entire edifice of theses collapses.

3. MODAL COLLAPSE

The subsequent discussion will make use of the following *Modal Collapse Theorem* (due to J. J. MacIntosh 1984):

Let F be any propositional qualifier ("modality") obeying the following three principles:

  (C) $F(p \;\&\; q) \supset (Fp \;\&\; Fq)$ *Conjunction Principle*
  (V) $Fp \supset p$ *Veracity Principle*
  (P) $p \supset \Diamond Fp$ *Possibility Principle*[3]

Then: F characterizes all truths. That is, it will be provable that $p \supset Fp$ or equivalently $(\forall t)Ft$.
PROOF:

(1) $F(p \;\&\; \sim Fp) \supset (Fp \;\&\; F\sim Fp)$	from (C) via the substitution $\sim Fp/q$
(2) $F\sim Fp \supset \sim Fp$	from (V) via the substitution $\sim Fp/p$
(3) $\sim F(p \;\&\; \sim Fp)$	since (2) amounts to the negation of (1)'s consequent

(4) $\Box\sim F(p\ \&\ \sim Fp)$ from (3) by necessitation
(5) $\sim\Diamond F(p\ \&\ \sim Fp)$ from (4) by modal logic
(6) $(p\ \&\ \sim Fp) \supset \Diamond F(p\ \&\ \sim Fp)$ from (P) via the sub-situation $(p\ \&\ \sim Fp)/p$
(7) $\sim(p\ \&\ \sim Fp)$ from (5), (6)
(8) $p \supset Fp$ from (7) Q.E.D.

Given both (C) and (V), we have, in effect derived $(\forall t)Ft$ from $(\forall t)\Diamond Ft$.

4. THE KNOWABILITY THESIS IN TROUBLE

The Modal Collapse Theorem can now be put to work via the specification:

$$Fp = (\exists x)Kxp$$

Observe that now (P) amounts to:

$$(\forall t)\Diamond(\exists x)Kxt \text{ or equivalently } \sim(\exists t)\Box(\forall x)\sim Kxt$$

which is to say that (P) comes to thesis IV. Seeing that (C) and (V) both obviously obtain with this present construal of F, the Modal Collapse Theorem yields:

$$(\forall t)(\exists x)Kxt$$

Since this IV-consequence to the effect that all truths are known is clearly unacceptable, so is IV itself.

This finding at one stroke invalidates the entire quartet at issue in the thesis spectrum of section 1. As already adumbrated above, the knowability thesis is unacceptable in all its forms. In particular, it follows from not-IV that with finite knowers there will be truths that no one can know possibly to be such.

5. FITCH'S THEOREM AND ITS IMPORT

The preceding findings on unknowability have interesting ramifications. Thus consider yet another application of the Modal Collapse Theorem, namely that arising with the following specification of F:

$$Fp = Kxp$$

The theorem's grounding principles (of Conjunction and Veracity) now both obtain once again, so that we have it that:

$$\text{If } (\forall t)\Diamond Kxt, \text{ then } (\forall t)Kxt$$

Now one certainly does not have it in general that:

$$\text{If } (\forall u)\Diamond Fu \text{ then } (\forall u)Fu$$

In this light the aforementioned implication thesis is aberrant and may seem surprising.

The implication thesis at issue initially established in Fitch (1963)—might be called Fitch's Theorem. To all intents and purposes it says that if every truth is *possibly* known to someone then every truth is *actually* known to this individual. So insofar as one is minded to deny the latter—as one surely must if God is to be put aside in our logical deliberations—the former has to be rejected as well. Accordingly $(\exists x)(\forall t)\Diamond Kxt$ must be rejected so that we have:

$$(\forall x)(\exists t)\Box \sim Kxt$$

On this basis, every knower is necessarily imperfect through there being some truth that is necessarily not known to him.

Fitch's Theorem should not really be seen as all that surprising. For suppose x is a limited knower. Then $(\exists t)\sim Kxt$. So let t_0 be such a truth that x does not know: $\sim Kxt_0$. And now consider the truth: $t_0 \ \& \sim Kxt_0$. Clearly x cannot possibly know *this* truth since $Kx(t_0 \ \& \sim Kxt_0)$ is self-contradictory. So we have it that $(\exists t)\sim \Diamond Kxt$. But observe that we have now effectively established $(\exists t)\sim Kxt \vdash (\exists t)\sim \Diamond Kxt$ or equivalently (by contraposition) $(\forall t)\Diamond Kxt \vdash (\forall t)Kxt$ Q.E.D.

Observe further Fitch's Theorem has the consequence

$$(\forall t)\Diamond Kxt \vdash \Diamond(\forall t)Kxt$$

whose generic analogue

$$(\forall u)\Diamond Fu \vdash \Diamond(\forall u)Fu$$

certainly does not obtain.

Fitch's Theorem does *not*, of course, mean that we have the clearly untenable:

$$(\forall t)(\forall K)(\Diamond Kxt \supset Kxt)$$

Nor yet does it mean that we have

$$(\forall t)[(\exists x)\Diamond Kxt \supset (\exists x)Kxt]^4$$

But what it does accomplish by way of a transit from possibility to actuality nevertheless has an anomalous air about it.

But be this as it may, since we have little alternative but to reject $(\exists x)(\forall t)Kxt$, Fitch's Theorem means that we have no alternative but also to reject:

$$(\exists x)(\forall t)\Diamond Kxt$$

And so we must accept its negation:

$$(\forall x)(\exists t)\sim\Diamond Kxt \text{ or equivalently } (\forall x)(\exists t)\Box\sim Kxt$$

For every finite knower there is something unknowable—some person-specific unknowable fact that this individual cannot know. All limited knowers have cognitive blind spots: for every finite knower there is some person-correlative unknowable—a truth that this individual cannot possibly know.[5] And of course the *conjunction* of all of these will yield a truth that no one can possibly know. The existence of unknowables is thus demonstrated as a matter of general principle.

Fitch's Theorem in effect establishes a collective incompatibility among the following four theses:

(F) Knower Finitude
     $(\forall x)(\exists t)\sim Kxt$

(C) The Conjunction Principle
     $Kx(p \mathbin{\&} q) \supset (Kxp \mathbin{\&} Kxq)$

(V) The Veracity Principle
     $Kxp \supset p$

(K) The Knowability Principle

$p \supset \Diamond Kxp$ or equivalently $(\forall t)\Diamond Kxt$

Accordingly, one or another of these plausible-seeming theses must be rejected. This situation is sometimes characterized as "Fitch's Paradox."[6]

However, our present treatment of epistemic logic does not see this situation as paradoxical but rather as a token of not implausible circumstance that for the reasons of the already indicted sort (K), the Knowability Principle, must be abandoned.

REFERENCES

Fitch, Frederic B. "A Logical Analysis of Some Value Concepts." *The Journal of Symbolic Logic* 28 (1963): 135–42.

Hart, W. D. "The Epistemology of Abstract Objects." *Proceedings of the Aristotelian Society*, Supplementary 53 (1979): 53–65.

MacIntosh, J. J. "Fitch's Features." *Analysis* 44 (1984): 153–58.

———. *Epistemic Logic.* Pittsburgh: University of Pittsburgh Press, 2005.

Rescher, Nicholas. *The Limits of Science.* (Blackwells and Los Angeles: University of California Press, 1984), 150n (second revised edition, Pittsburgh: University of Pittsburgh Press, 1999).

Routley, Richard. "Necessary Limits to Knowledge: Unknown Truths." In *Essays in Scientific Philosophy*, ed. by E. Morscher et al. Bad Reichenhall: Comes, 1981, 93–113.

Williamson, Timothy. "Intuitionism Disproved?" *Analysis* 42 (1982): 203–7.

———. "Knowability and Constructivism" *Philosophical Quarterly* 38 (1988): 422–43.

———. "On Knowledge and the Unknowable." *Analysis* 42 (1987): 203–7.

———. "On the Paradox of Knowability." *Mind* 96 (1987): 154–58.

NOTES

1. This terrain at large is canvassed in several recent books including Rescher (1985) and Williamson (2000).

2. Note that the structurally cognate thesis

$$\Diamond(\forall t)(\forall x)Kxt \text{ or equivalently } \Diamond(\forall x)(\forall t)Kxt$$

to the effect that possibly everyone is omniscient is ruled out by our focus upon finite knowers. And its weaker cousin $\Diamond(\forall t)(\exists x)Kxt$ maintaining the possibility that every truth known by someone or other can also be ruled out. Since every member of our finite population of knowers has a secret, the *conjunction* of all of these is a proposition that it is not possible for anyone to know.

3. Since we suppose that F is (as a *propositional* qualifier) is closed under logical equivalence, $Fp \supset p$ is equivalent with $p \supset \sim F \sim p$, thesis (V) comes to $(\forall t) \sim F \sim t$. And of course (P) comes to $(\forall t)\Diamond Ft$.

4. Let it be that x is the only person ever in a position to learn a certain fact say by being "the last man on earth" but that his attention is otherwise engaged.

5. On this issue see Sorensen (1988) and Daniels (1988).

6. For the relevant literature see the bibliography.

Bibliography

Allen, Thomas Barton. *The Quest: A Report on Extraterrestrial Life.* Philadelphia: Chilton Books, 1965.

Anderson, Paul. *Is There Life on Other Worlds?* New York and London: Collier-Macmillan, 1963.

Anonymous. "The Future as Suggested by Developments of the Past Seventy-Five Years." *Scientific American* 123 (1920): 321.

Ball, John A. "Extraterrestrial Intelligence: Where Is Everybody?" *American Scientist* 68 (1980): 565–663.

———. "The Zoo Hypothesis." *Icarus* 19 (1973): 347–49.

Beall, J. C., ed. *Liars and Heaps: New Essays on Paradox.* Oxford: Clarendon Press, 2003.

Beck, Lewis White. "Extraterrestrial Intelligent Life." *Proceedings and Addresses of the American Philosophical Association* 45 (1971–1972): 5–21.

Berrill, N. J. *Worlds Without End.* London: Macmillan, 1964.

Bohm, David. *Causality and Chance in Modern Physics.* London: Routledge, 1957.

Bracewell, Ronald N. *The Galactic Club: Intelligent Life in Outer Space.* San Francisco: W. H. Freeman, 1975.

Breuer, Reinhard. *Contact With The Stars.* Trans. by C. Payne-Gaposchkin and M. Lowery. New York: W. H. Freeman, 1982.

Burns, L. *Vagueness: An Investigation into Natural Languages and the Sorites Paradox.* Dordrecht: Reidel, 1991.

Cameron, A. G. W., ed. *Interstellar Communication: A Collection of Reprints and Original Contributions.* New York and Amsterdam: W. A. Benjamin, 1963.

Cassirer, Ernst. *Determinism and Indeterminism in Modern Physics: Historical and Systematic Studies of the Problem of Causality.* New Haven: Yale University Press, 1956.

Chaitin, Gregory J. *The Unknowable.* Singapore and New York: Springer, 1999.

Dick, Steven J. *Plurality of Worlds: The Origins of the Extraterrestrial Life Debate from Democritus to Kant.* Cambridge: Cambridge University Press, 1982.

Diogenes Laertius. *Lives of the Philosophers.*

Dole, Stephen H. *Habitable Planets for Man.* New York: Blaisdell, 1964; 2nd ed., New York: American Elsevier, 1970.

Dole, Stephen H., and Iassc Asimov. *Planets for Man.* New York: Random House, 1964.

Drake, Frank D. *Intelligent Life in Space.* New York and London: Macmillan, 1962.

du Bois-Reymond. "The Limits of Our Knowledge of Nature." *Popular Science Monthly* 5 (1874): 17–32.

———. *Über die Grenzen des Naturekennens: Die Sieben Welträtsel—Zwei Vorträge,* 11th ed. Leipzig: Veit & Co., 1916.

Ehrensvaerd, Goesta. *Man on Another World.* Chicago and London: University of Chicago Press, 1965.

Eiseley, Loren. *The Immense Journey.* New York: Random House, 1937.

Firsoff, V. A. *Life Beyond the Earth: A Study in Exobiology.* New York: Basic Books, 1963.

Fitch, Frederic B. "A Logical Analysis of Some Value Concepts." *The Journal of Symbolic Logic* 28 (1963): 135–42.

Gale, George. *Scientific American* 245 (December 1981): 154–71.

Gavvay, Allen. "Les Principes foundamenteaus de la conaissance: Le Modele des intelligenes extraterrêtres." *Science, Histoire, Épistémologie: Actes du Premier Colloque Européen d'Histoire et Philosophie des Sciences*. Paris: J. Vrin, 1981: 33–59.

Goclenius, Randolph. *Introduction to Aristotle's Organon. Isagoge in Organon Aristotelis*. Frankfurt, 1598.

Grim, Patrick. "There is No Set of All Truths." *Analysis* 44 (1984): 206–8.

Haeckel. *Die Welträtsel.*

Handler, Philip, ed. *Biology and the Future of Man*. Oxford: Oxford University Press, 1970.

Handy, Rollo. "Haeckel, Ernst Heinrich." In *The Encyclopedia of Philosophy*, ed. by Paul Edwards, vol. III. New York: Macmillan, 1967.

Hart, M. H. "An Explanation for the Absence of Extraterrestrials on Earth." *Quarterly Journal of the Royal Astronomical Society* 16 (1975): 128–35.

Hart, W. D. "The Epistemology of Abstract Objects." *Proceedings of the Aristotelian Society*, Supplementary 53 (1979): 53–65.

Hempel, Carl G. "Science Unlimited." *Annals of the Japan Association for Philosophy of Science* 14 (1973): 200.

Herrmann, Joachim. *Leven auf anderen Sternen*. Guetersloh: Bertelsmann Verlag, 1963.

Hoyle, Fred. *The Black Cloud*. New York: Harper, 1957.

———. *Of Men and Galaxies*. Seattle: University of Washington Press, 1966.

Huang, Su-Shu. "Life Outside the Solar System." *Scientific American* 202, 4 (April 1960): 55–63.

Hugly, Philip, and Charles Sayward. "Can a Language Have Indenumerably Many Expressions?" *History and Philosophy of Logic* (1983).

Hume, David. *Dialogues Concerning Natural Religion*. Ed. by N. K. Smith. London, 1920.

Huygens, Christiaan. *Cosmotheoros: The Celestial Worlds Discovered—New Conjectures Concerning the Planetary Worlds, Their Inhabitants and Productions*. London: F. Cass & Co., 1968.

James, William. *Pragmatism*. New York: Longmans, 1907.

Jeans, Sir James. "Is There Life in Other Worlds?" A 1941 Royal Institution lecture reprinted in H. Shapley et al., eds. *Readings in the Physical Sciences*. New York: Appleton-Century-Crofts, 1948: 112–17.

Jevons, W. Stanley. *The Principles of Science*, 2nd ed. London: Macmillan, 1874.

Kaplan, S. A., ed. *Extraterrestrial Civilization: Problems of Interstellar Communication*. Jerusalem: Israel Program for Scientific Translations, 1971.

Kuhn, Thomas. *The Structure of Scientific Revolution*. Chicago: University of Chicago Press, 1962.

Leibniz, G. W. "Principles de la nature et de la grace."

Lem, S. *Summa Technologiae*. Krakow: Wyd. Lt., 1964.

Leslie, John. "Anthropic Principle, World Ensemble, Design." *American Philosophical Quarterly* 19 (1982): 141–51.

———. "Efforts to Explain All Existence." *Mind* 87 (1978): 181–97.

———. "The Theory that the World Exists Because It Should." *American Philosophical Quarterly* 7 (1910): 286–98.

———. *Value and Existence*. Totowa, N.J.: Rowman & Littlefield, 1979.

———. "The World's Necessary Existence." *International Journal for the Philosophy of Religion* 11 (1980): 297–329.

MacGowan, Roger A., and Frederick Ordway. "On the Possibilities of the Existence of Extraterrestrial Intelligence." In *Advances in Space Science and Technology*, ed. by F. I. Ordway. New York and London: Academic Press, 1962: 4:39–111.

———. *Intelligence in the Universe*. Englewood Cliffs, N.J.: Prentice Hall, 1966.

MacIntosh, J. J. "Fitch's Features." *Analysis* 44 (1984): 153–58.

McCabe. *The Riddle of the Universe—At the Close of the Nineteenth Century*. New York and London: Harper & Bros., 1901.

McCord Adams, Mary. *William Ockham*, vol. II. Notre Dame, Ind.: University of Notre Dame Press, 1987.

McGee, V. *Truth, Vagueness, and Paradox*. Indianapolis: Hackett, 1990.

McMullin, Ernan. "Review of Robert Nozick 'R.S.V.P.—A Story.'" *Icarus* 14 (1971): 291–94.

Nagel, Thomas. "What Is It Like to Be a Bat?" *Mortal Questions*. Cambridge, Mass.: Harvard University Press, 1976.

Nozick, Robert. *Philosophical Explanations*. Cambridge, Mass.: Harvard University Press, 1981.

———. "R.S.V.P.—A Story." *Commentary* 53 (1972): 66–68.

Peirce, Charles Sanders. *Collected Papers*. Ed. by C. Hartshorne et al., vol. VI. Cambridge, Mass.: Harvard University Press, 1929.

Prantl. *Geschichte der Logik im Abendlande.*

Pucetti, Roland. *Persons: A Study of Possible Moral Agents in the Universe*. New York: Herder and Herder, 1969.

Purcell, E. *Interstellar Communication: A Collection of Reprints and Original Contributions*. Ed. by A. G. W. Cameron. New York and Amsterdam: W. A. Benjamin, 1963.

Rescher, Nicholas. *Epistemic Logic*. Pittsburgh: University of Pittsburgh Press, 2005.

———. *Kant and the Reach of Reason: Studies in Kant's Theory of Rational Systematization*. Cambridge: Cambridge University Press, 2000.

———. *The Limits of Science*. Blackwells and Los Angeles: University of California Press, 1984.

———. *Paradoxes*. Chicago: Open Court, 2001.

Rood, Robert T., and James S. Trefil. *Are We Alone: The Possibility of Extraterrestrial Civilization*. New York: Scribners, 1981.

Routley, Richard. "Necessary Limits to Knowledge: Unknown Truths." In E. *Essays in Scientific Philosophy*, ed. by E. Morscher et al. Bad Reichenhall: Comes, 1981: 93–113.

Rowe, William. *The Cosmological Argument*. Princeton: Princeton University Press, 1975.

Sagan, Carl. *The Cosmic Connection*. New York: Doubleday, 1973.

———. *Cosmos.* New York: Random House, 1980.

Sainsbury, R. M. *Paradoxes.* 2nd ed. Cambridge: Cambridge University Press, 1995.

Shapley, Harlow. *Of Stars and Men.* Boston: Beacon Press, 1958.

Shklovskii, I. S., and Carl Sagan. *Intelligent Life in the Universe.* San Francisco: Holden-Day, 1966.

Simmel, Georg. "Uber eine Beziehung der Kelektionslehre zur Erkenntnistheorie." *Archiv für systematische Philosophie und Soziologie* 1 (1895): 34–45.

Simpson, George Gaylord. "The Nonprevalence of Humanoids." *Science* 143 (1964): 769–75.

Sorensen, Roy E. *Blindspots.* Oxford: Clarendon Press, 1988.

Strawson, P. F. "Truth." *Proceedings of the Aristotelian Society,* Supplementary 24 (1950): 129–56.

Sullivan, Walter. *We Are Not Alone.* New York: McGraw Hill, 1964; rev. ed., 1965.

von Hoerner, Sevastian. "Astronomical Aspects of Interstellar Communication." *Astronautica Acta* 18 (1973): 421–29.

Whorf, Benjamin Lee. "Language and Logic." In *Language, Thought, and Reality,* ed. by J. B. Carroll. Cambridge, Mass.: 1956: 240–41.

Williamson, Timothy. "Intuitionism Disproved?" *Analysis* 42 (1982): 203–7.

———. "Knowability and Constructivism." *Philosophical Quarterly* 38 (1988): 422–43.

———. "On Knowledge and the Unknowable." *Analysis* 42 (1987): 203–7.

———. "On the Paradox of Knowability." *Mind* 96 (1987): 154–58.

Wittgenstein, Ludwig. *Tractatus.*

Zeller, Edward. *Philosophie der Griechen.*

Ziman, John. *Reliable Knowledge.* Cambridge: Cambridge University Press, 1969.

Index

About the Author

NICHOLAS RESCHER was born in Hagen, Germany, in 1928 and came to the United States at the age of ten. He attended Queens College in New York City and earned his doctorate at Princeton in 1951 while still at the age of twenty-two—a record for Princeton's Department of Philosophy. Since 1961 he has been at the University of Pittsburgh where he is Distinguished University Professor. He has served as Chairman of the Department of Philosophy and is Chairman of the Center for Philosophy of Science.

In a productive research career extending over six decades, Rescher has established himself as a systematic philosopher of the old style and author of a system of pragmatic idealism which weaves together threads of thought from continental idealism and American pragmatism. And apart from this larger program Rescher's many-sided work has made significant contributions to logic (the conception autodescriptive systems of many-sided logic), to the history of logic (the medieval Arabic theory of modal syllogistic), to the theory of knowledge (epistemetrics as a quantitative approach in theoretical epistemology), to the philosophy of science (in particular it its economic aspects and as regards the relation of science and religion). Rescher has also worked in the area of futuristics, and along with Olaf Helmer and Norman Dalkey is co-inaugurator of the so-called Delphi method of forecasting. And the Encyclopedia of Bioethics credits Rescher with writing one of the very first articles in the field. Seventeen of Rescher's books have been translated into eight other languages.

One of the first among the increasing number of contemporary exponents of philosophical idealism, Rescher has been active in the rehabilitation of the coherence theory of truth and in the reconstruction of philosophical pragmatism in line with the idealistic tradition. He has pioneered the development of inconsistency-tolerant logics and, in the philosophy of science, the logarithmic retardation theory of scientific progress based on the epistemological principle that our knowledge in a field does not increase in proportion with the volume of information but only with its logarithm. Some dozen books about Rescher's work have appeared in English, German, and Italian and Arabic. His contributions to philosophy have been recognized by honorary degrees awarded by eight universities on three continents.

For over three decades Rescher has been editor of the *American Philosophical Quarterly*. The author of more than seventy books in various areas of philosophy, works by Mr. Rescher have been translated into German, Spanish, French, Italian, and Japanese. He has lectured at universities in many countries, and has occupied visiting posts at various universities in North America and Europe (including Oxford, Konstanz, and Salamanca). He has held fellowships from the J. S. Guggenheim Foundation, the Ford Foundation, and the American Philosophical Society. A former president of the American Philosophical Association (Eastern Division), of the American Catholic Philosophical Association, of the American Metaphysical Society, of the C. S. Peirce Society, and of the G. W. Leibniz Society of America. Rescher has also served as member of the Board of Directors of the International Federation of Philosophical Societies, an organ of UNESCO.

An honorary member of Corpus Christi College, Oxford, Rescher has been elected to membership in the European Academy of Arts and Sciences (Academia Europaea), The Royal Society of Canada, the Institut International de Philosophie, and the Academie Internationale de Philosophie des Sciences. Having held visiting lectureships at Oxford, Constance, Salamanca, Munich, and Marburg, he has been awarded fellowships by the Ford, Guggenheim, and National Science Foundations. Author of some hundred books ranging over many areas of philosophy, over a dozen of them translated from English into other languages. In 1977 its fellow elected him an honorary member of Corpus Christi College, Oxford, and in 1983 he received an Alexander von Humboldt Humanities Prize, awarded under the auspices of the Federal Republic of Germany "in recognition of the research accomplishments of humanistic scholars of international distinction." In 2005 he was awarded the Beligian Cardinal Mercier Prize and in 2006 he was awarded the Thomas Aquinas Medal of the American Catholic Philosophical Association.

Rescher has been commissioned to undertake support studies for Congressional committees on science/technology matters and has been invited to testify before Committee on Science and Technology on issues of space exploration and colonization. He belongs to a family that has been prolific in scholars and scientists, including the eminent orientalist Oskar Rescher.

Made in the USA
Middletown, DE
01 February 2017